PATCHWORK SCRAPBOOK

One Woman's Midlife Search For Self
Told Through Her Quilts, Poems and Essays

Carla Rodio

ISBN- 978-0-692-73830-06

Library of Congress Control Number: 2016914047

Patchwork Scrapbook
One Woman's Midlife Search fo Self Told Through Her Quilts, Poems and Essays

Printed in the U.S.A.

Bootstrap Publishing
mkd@bootstrappublishing.net

BOOK SECTIONS

Along the Mohawk

banner

I

First Steps

Along the Mohawk: banner

First Steps

Betrayed

Nebula: kite wall hanging

Fledgeling

Journey

Awakening

Call of the Muse

Crafting

Sunrise

The Other Side of Darkness

First Steps

It was a giant step for change when I requested a leave of absence from teaching kindergarten. Some people find direction for their lives at an early age. By midlife I needed to find what I really wanted to do. It wasn't a smooth journey. There were bumps and detours and getting lost. Like the kite in my fledgling poem, I spent a lot of time seeking and reaching for the right direction and often crashing. Over the years, I've discovered untapped resources inside myself, gained new knowledge, skills and insights I could use to help me on my way. There were experiences, people and sights, I would have never have known if I had stayed teaching until retirement.

During the Bicentennial people were honoring the crafts and ethics of former times. Many were making quilts. My first step in a new direction was taking a quilt class during summer vacation. Making something so practical and at the same time beautiful out of scraps of cloth was powerful. I wanted to know more. Many thanks go to my husband who encouraged me to attend Fiberworks School for the Textile Arts in Berkeley, California and later move to North Carolina from upstate New York.

At Fiberworks, there were classes and workshops for stitching, spinning, weaving and dyeing. I learned how cloth is made and decorated in many places and cultures worldwide. My most important job was planning a career with the help of my adviser. My plan succeeded. I had a shop where quilting supplies were sold and I could teach quiltmaking. But there seemed to be more I had to do. North Carolina was beckoning to me.

North Carolina honors crafts and the people who practice them. In the western part of the state are two well known craft centers, Penland and the John C. Campbell School. They were founded to preserve and teach the crafts of the early settlers. The State Council for the Arts has offices in every county. They promote all the arts and crafts through grants, programs and exhibits. It offers the Mountain Arts Program, a roster of artists and craftspeople who teach their specialties in mountain schools. It was a privilege for me to be part of this program. I taught hands on quiltmaking in many of the mountain elementary schools while I continued creating patchwork wall hangings.

Blue Ridge Community College and the University of North Carolina in Asheville offered classes to adult learners. I attended computer, writing and drawing classes where I gained new skills and knowledge. In the process I found my muse. There was no path to follow. It was a time of looking, listening and learning what I could do. These poems and essays were written during my journey to find myself. They are a record of my self-discovery.

Betrayed

Betrayed
by her own
indolence
insecurity
and lack of
independence

She waited
for life to
come
to her
to happen

Life happened
it happened
all around her
it happened
for others
they made it
happen

She waited
for life to
come
to her
to happen

Betrayed by
her own
indolence
insecurity
and lack of
independence

Nebula

Kite Wall Hanging

Fledgling

Faltering
until a gust lifts it higher
like a dry leaf
seeking, turning
on flowing layers of air currents

Pent up spirit
pulling, tugging to be free
reaching for clouds
searching for liberation

Swinging and dipping
in the ocean of air
over tree tops
and electric wires
daring the wind

Sucked into a fatal spiral
plunging in a sudden
down draft
a mighty kite flight ends.

Journey

Was it you stirring in early morning light
or just a breeze fluttering my mind awake
after a night visiting memories populated
by family and friends, mementos of work,
trips, concerts, pictures, books, receipts,
projects done-not done, things said-not said

No return, map or traveler guidebook
available for this memorable expedition
packed with unusual encounters

Slogging through desert wastelands of despair
then frozen in wintry misunderstandings
climbing to heights of hopefulness and joy
slipping on the slopes of promises not kept
persevering to find the way and not stumble
looking for direction to the next viewpoint.

Awakening

Faithfully as a tree grows
deep strong roots
I reach into my soul
to explore the truth
in this dark, dark night.

What to do with my thoughts?
What would my friends think?
Must I explore the truth?
I rise from the earth and shout,
Will I grow with experience?

Call of the Muse

The call of the muse
is not to all the same

Some put brush to canvas
lips to horn
chisel to stone
bow to strings
toe to floor

Compelled to do it
driven to create
some inner force
pushing
every fiber of being

Creating a gift
a treasure
to show
exposed to all
to witness

The call of the muse
is not to all the same

Crafting

If I were to
collect fragments of
thoughts and scraps
of colorful words
to patch together
with
threads of meaning
spread across
a vacant page
for your pleasure.

Sunrise

We see
from the plane
at dawn
mountain tops
become islands
in a sea of
morning fog
flowing between
ridges,
to be caught
like snow
in valley crevices

The Other Side of Darkness

Sometimes things are so dark you can't see to the other side, like when there's a storm and you're out in it driving on slick wet tar covered roads in the mountains. You go slowly and let your instincts guide you through, even though your heart is racing and you don't know what's around the next bend. One night I took the shortcut back from the city. Even though I knew the back road well and never encountered anything before, I always geared down to second before descending into the curves. One of the curves was a hairpin. The sign at the crest before descending shows 25 mph. Shortly after the crest is the first curve. One side of the road borders an embankment. The other side drops steeply to a tangle of trees and vines. No guard fence rail there. This particular night, as soon as I was into the first curve, I found a small truck blocking my lane of the two-lane road. Front end up the embankment and rear end across my lane. A man staggered and fell from the driver's door as I stopped. Stopping was not a good idea because someone could come round the curve and ram into the rear of my small car. I pulled around the wreck and back to my side to yell back to him that I would call for help from home.

"Don't do that. I don't want no sheriff." For my own safety, I left and hoped no one would be hurt.

But what did it mean to me? After all these years I wonder if I was at a point in my history that meant for me to wonder what I was doing and where I was going in my life. Sometimes people mess up because they can't see to the other side. It's easy to see where you've been. The hard part is looking ahead to see where you're going. Sometimes it can be too dark to see very far. That's when you gotta slow down to get around the next bend in the road.

Splendor

wall hanging

II

Quilts

Splendor: wall hanging

Storage

Cut, Piece, Sew

A Full Closet

A Quilter's Philosophy

Community Quilt

A Southern Appalachian Exhibit

A Quilt for All Ages: wall hanging

How a Five Month Old Baby Helped Make a Quilt

Six Million Stars *Wall Hanging*

Six Million Stars

Banners for the Earth

Henderson County Earth Day Quilt: wall hanging

Storage

Closets enclose,
Closets contain,
Closets retain
Old and new
Fit and unfit
Fair and ugly
Useless trash??
Neverrr
Contents remain

Concealed
Memories
Never revealed
Like stories
Old and new
Fit and unfit
Fair and ugly
Useless trash??
Neverrr
Contents remain

Collect and store
Up to ceiling
Down to floor
Garnering
Old and new,
Fit and unfit,
Fair and ugly
Useless trash???
Maybe
Contents remain.

Cut, Piece, Sew

Weaving dreams
among fabrics
plain and bold

her first quilt
a passion of
new found
knowledge

now a
tattered, old
archeological
treasure

r-r-rip the chain
of stitches.
Cut, piece and sew

fresh dreams
of quilts
to grow old.

A Full Closet

When my husband wanted to regain the use of a closet, I was propelled into quilt- making. For years I had been saving scraps of fabric from my home sewing projects in this closet. At first, it was a single shelf in the closet, but as time went by, the fabric scraps occupied more and more space until it was filled to capacity. Each time I sewed something, I would tell my family, "Someday I will make a quilt out of these beautiful pieces" of cloth.

In preparation for a summer vacation to a Road Island Beach, I had subscribed to the local newspaper. It was my husband, Fran, who read the issue that published the patchwork quiltmaking class announcement. "Here's your chance to make something from all your scrap fabric and I could get to use the closet again," he suggested. I looked at the announcement and learned that the class was at night. I wouldn't lose any beach time during the day. Why not? I thought.

The first class was exciting and satisfying. I learned to use my sewing skills to merge geometric forms with a variety of colors. I felt that I was uniting the talents of both my parents. My mother was an artist who studied at the national Academy of Design and the Art Students League. Her work exposed me to creativity, resourcefulness, and the elements of art. My father was a civil engineer. His work made me aware of the geometry and mathematical precision necessary for a structure to stand. I could see that quiltmaking involved all these elements. It made me want to learn more about this craft. I took classes, attended textile school, and was certified as a quilting instructor. All this led me to a career change from being an elementary teacher to teaching about quiltmaking.

I've enjoyed helping many people learn about patchwork. I've worked with all ages from five to ninety-five. There are many group quilts in western North Carolina that I helped create, a collaborative venture requiring cooperation, respect, and dedication for the successful completion of the project. In the end, there is always a sense of satisfaction and accomplishment and appreciation for all involved. It's like conducting an orchestra. Everyone shares the pleasure of the concert: the audience, musicians, and a conductor. In addition, there's a tangible piece of work to behold as often as you like.

Oh yes, about that closet. It never really emptied out. I've continued to buy more beautiful pieces of cloth to cut up and make more patchwork.

A Quilter's Philosophy

People frequently question the validity of showing quilts in an art gallery. Are quilts a craft that someone is trying to elevate to an art form by displaying them in areas traditionally reserved for painting or sculpture? Historically, quilting has been considered a craft that has been useful to many people all over the world. Today, we rarely need to make a quilt for utilitarian purposes, so we have started to hang quilts on the wall. In doing so, we have begun to see many of these quilts as exciting graphic designs.

I have come to realize that my quiltmaking is not the creation of traditional quilts that people have made in the past. However, traditional techniques and designs from the past form the basis of my work. The form is very geometric and needs to be held together visually and physically. At present I am experimenting with and studying color. My palette is limited to the fabrics sold over the store counter. Working through color and design problems in creating pieces has been valuable in my development as a fiber artist. It has given me the courage to experiment and be inventive. I hope my work will be seen as creations of the second half of the twentieth century.

Lately, my pieces have been created on a flannel-covered wall. Pieces of fabric cling to the surface of the cloth. In "Splendor," I wanted to create the illusion of light and space through the use of color. It was easy to move the triangles around, and I could stand back from my work surface to observe from a distance what I had done. This was much like a painter's use of an easel. It gave me the feeling that I was having a dialogue with my work. Quiltmaking so far has been a grand adventure. I feel like an explorer who has been discovering new and beautiful territories.

From the program for my one-person show at Utica College, ©1984.

Community Quilt

The morning of May 7th was clear and bloomed into a hot, sunny day. A perfect backdrop for the Fifth Annual Art Festival sponsored by the Henderson County Four Seasons Arts Council. The yearly fete is a mixture of a medieval fair and an all-American holiday picnic. Musicians, dancers and magicians wove amongst the exhibits, featuring art and photographs. Fun and merriment were the order of the day, and amongst it all, we quilters were there, helping people create crazy patchwork blocks for the Community Quilt.

In preparation for the day, a core group of quilters practiced doing the planned activity several weeks in advance. Supplies were solicited and donated by individuals and local businesses: cloth scraps, fabric for lining, batting, Pellon, thread, marking pens, crochet cotton as well as people's time and talent were generously given, and volunteers helped prepare the materials to be used by the participants.

Three-year-old children and great-grandmothers, young and old couples, mothers and daughters (or sons), fathers and sons (or daughters) helped to fashion 140 quilt blocks. Pleasure, and satisfaction in the experience were evident in the expressions of all who participated. It was an opportunity for quilt-makers to share the art of quiltmaking with the general public. People who have always wanted to make a quilt could realize making some of this one. Children ran to find relatives and friends to show them their blocks on a large board in back of our work area. Others watched with fascination as their blocks were pressed, machine-stitched, and hung. There was excitement and joy for all involved.

Many of the volunteers stayed well beyond their allotted time, helping enthusiastic participants create their blocks, press the designs on iron-on Pellon, zigzag stitch the raw edges, clip threads, and trim squares. The success of this project is due to the dedication of these women and the others who donated and prepared the materials.

Participants signed each block and a special book with a laundry-marking pen. Later, all the collected blocks were sewn together and a border added. A quilting bee was held to tie the quilt, which was bound and prepared for hanging. During the Apple Festival at the end of August 1988, the finished quilt was presented to the mayor. It will hang in the lobby of City Hall for all to see and remain a historic reminder of the energy, talents, and cooperation of so many people in the community.

A Southern Appalachian Exhibit

The last rays of daylight shifted with the evening shadows to establish the magic of the familiar misty mountain views as I drove to the opening for the "We the Quilters" exhibition. It was being held in the gallery of the Folk Art Center, which is nestled in a woodsy setting at milepost 32 on the Blue Ridge Parkway, just east of Asheville, North Carolina. The purpose of the regional competitions leading up to this exhibition was to foster awareness, knowledge and appreciation of the Constitution during the bicentennial years of 1986-1989. It was made possible through a grant from the Appalachian Regional Commission. Individuals and groups from all Counties in the thirteen Appalachian states were eligible to enter. This included Alabama, Georgia, Kentucky, Maryland, Mississippi, New York, North Carolina, Ohio, Pennsylvania, South Carolina, Tennessee, Virginia, and West Virginia.

As I reached the Art Center parking lot, I saw many out-of-state license plates. I assumed some belonged to exhibitors. I wasn't disappointed. The first person I met was Lois Smith of Rockville, Maryland. She had driven to Asheville in her camper that day to enjoy the festivities. Her winning quilt was a sampler made as a wedding gift for her son and daughter-in-law, and aptly named "Heritage". The quilt signifies the Smith family history and traditions in twenty-five pieced and appliqued blocks with traditional designs used in unique ways. Among them was an eight pointed star design used for the Smith family Christmas tree. In another block she had appliqued spools of thread to honor all the needle workers in her family.

As I backed up to photograph the Maryland/Smith quilt, I literally bumped into Margaret Young Yates, the creator of the Kentucky quilt. She had used the English piecing technique to stitch thirteen five half inch blocks, which resembled sections of a stained glass window. Each of the blocks show-cased a color of the state flag it represented. She found the designs for these blocks in the 1907 "Hearth and Homes" magazine. An appliqued map of the thirteen ratifying states appeared to be tacked to a window frame. A border fabric wallpaper of that period1 completed the piece.

I found Carol Bitt of Wytheville, Virginia, whose medallion quilt in red, white and blue was titled "The Three Branches". Carol felt challenged to create a quilt using only patchwork. The center block symbolizes the White House for the Executive branch; the side center blocks represent the Legislative branch; and the cornerstone blocks are the Courthouse Steps design for the judicial branch. It took 1,263 triangles to create the outside border. The continuous border signifies our nation's continuing form of government. Carol quilted the names of the thirteen original states in the inside border and fifty stars in the outside border.

Mingling happily alongside the victorious quilt-makers were friends, proud relatives, guests, and James Gentry, the Project Manager and Director for this exhibition. He is also the Director of the Folk Art Center and accepted the responsibility for promoting and installing the exhibit. An exhibition program for the quilts has been scheduled through January 1989 at folk-art centers and galleries in Alabama, North Carolina, South Carolina, Mississippi, and Georgia. Present were members of the Appalachian Regional Commission including Laura Edson of the Commission who conceived the idea of the quilt exhibit as the organization's project for the Constitutional Bicentennial.

This exhibit was truly a patchwork of people, places, and organizations, tying together so much of what makes our country unique: our Constitution, American quiltmaking, and most important the people. Conceived for the people, by the people and of the people, "We the Quilters" was truly an event in the spirit of the Constitution.

This article appeared in Country Quilts magazine, Summer 1988

A Quilt for All Ages

wall hanging

How a Five Month Old Baby Helped to Make a Quilt

It was Christmas, and the whole family was together. We hadn't been together for a long time and no one knew when we might get together again. Something special had to be done to remember this time.

Grandma said, "Since I know a lot about quiltmaking, let's create some patchwork. Each one will make a quilt block."

Everybody was given a white cloth square. Each one had to lay a yellow cloth strip diagonally on the white square. Then they could cover the rest of the square with whatever they chose from the scrap basket. Everybody got to work. Each one made a patchwork square. Even Eric, just three years old, made one. Everybody signed his or her names on their own patchwork square. The squares were set together and turned so the yellow strips connected. This linked all the blocks together.

But there was one person in the family who had not made a quilt square. Too small and young, Laura was just a baby. At five months old, she didn't know what Eric knew. She didn't understand how to make a patchwork square. She could do baby things: eat, sleep, cry, and play. She didn't know how to make a square. But she was part of the family. She belonged in the quilt. How could that happen? The family thought and thought. Then the idea came to us. You know how a baby keeps its hand in a fist? Very gently, we opened her fist and spread-open her fingers. She didn't like it. We laid her hands on a piece of cloth and traced around her thumb, forefinger, middle finger, ring finger, and tiny little baby finger. We took the outline of her hand to the sewing machine and stitched it. We made four stitched outlines of Laura's hand and each outline went in a corner of the family quilt.

Someday, Laura and Eric will be all grown up. They will have the family quilt. And it will remind them of a special time and special people in their lives.

Six Million Stars

wall hanging

Six Million Stars

The radio plays softly, as I work on patchwork in my studio, keeping me company, lulling my conscious mind and allowing the creative parts to flow. There are discussions, stories and music interspersed with news and weather. Sometimes I hear what is said. I hear that today is sunny and tomorrow it might rain. I learn that fighting is intensifying in Yugoslavia; Croats, Serbians, and Bosnians continue to maim and murder one another. I'm informed that 60% of American preschool children are not immunized against diseases that were virtually wiped out ten years ago. It is announced that Czechoslovakia has split into two nations. I am told that more people than ever watched the Super Bowl and that domestic violence is greater after such a sporting event. Great numbers of women and children starve to death in Somalia every day because there is no government. The story of one group persecuting another group of people seems to go on no matter what kind of weather we have. Jews know about that. The whole recorded history of Jews is long on tyranny.

My Six Million Stars wall hanging represents only one of many tyrannies consciously acted by one group of people against another. The various pieces of cloth represent clothing that people might have worn to the camps. Maybe they thought the wool would, at least, protect them from the cold. The six-pointed star (Magan David) is the motif of this piece. The basic element in the star is a 30° x 60° diamond shape. For me, the diamond translates into the form of a simple coffin. The diamonds are arranged to appear as tumbling blocks into what might be a pit. The lives of those suffering oppression have been so cheapened that they can be thrown away. It's like what we used to do with our refuse in our landfills. If we no longer have a use for it, we plow the refuse into the ground so it can decay, be forgotten. Hope lies in the ashes and the decomposed matter at the bottom of the heap. Perhaps it will one day constitute a new and different composition. On the right side, blood, fire, and anger rise and fall in an orange/red spurt. The only constancy is the twinkling of the distant stars in the void of space.

Banners For the Earth

All over the world, people have used scraps of cloth to patch clothing or to create larger pieces of fabric. It is part of a tradition that tells people to use it up, wear it out, or recycle. Quiltmaking is a craft born of this tradition, and it is most appealing in this environmentally conscious era. It is an important part of the North Carolina Mountain heritage as well. Therefore, it seems most appropriate to provide a patchwork activity during the 1990 Earth Day celebration in Henderson County, NC.

On Earth Day, a shelter in Jackson Park became our banner-making center. Materials were set on one table. There were muslin strips, marking pens, and Kool-Aid dye. Other Earth Day activities took place, and participants came from all over Henderson County to enjoy hikes, landscape painting, and recycling demonstrations. There were families or just friends together who wanted to learn the meaning of the day and participate in the many activities.

When people arrived at our shelter, they were invited to select a strip of cloth on which to inscribe a message or print with the dye. Some did both. They wrote about their hopes for a healthier planet and their love for the earth. They used their hands, leaves, and sticks to print and draw with the dye. There was an outpouring of wishes for a better world, a determination to help the environment and pledges to save the planet. Each muslin strip was tied to one of the little branches that had been pruned from my neighbor's apple tree. The branches were thrust into the ground. As the day progressed, a field of banners grew, softly fluttering whenever there was a breeze. That evening, the apple branches with their banners were set along the lakeshore at Blue Ridge Community College. Several people read and spoke about the meaning of our Earth Day. As the banners floated in the dusk, dancers wove among them. It was a time to reflect on a long and meaningful day.

Those muslin banners have become pledges to the earth by many people in Henderson County. In order to honor those pledges, they have now been made into a wall quilt. A quilt top was designed and pieced with the help of friends. The earth is in the center, the banners around it. In each of the four corners is a tree, representing the four seasons. Girls from several Brownie troops attended quilting bees, during which time they tied the three layers of the quilt together. More friends bound and finished the edges.

County residents and businesses donated all materials used in this quilt. Truly, it was a community wide effort that was in keeping with the time-honored tradition of people working together and helping each other for the good of the community. One lesson learned from the 1990 Earth Day is that every day is Earth Day. It is the responsibility of each and every one of us to preserve and protect the air, water, land, and all its inhabitants if life is to continue.

This Earth Day quilt belongs to the people of Henderson County, the ones who created it and those who come after them. It will hang where all can see it and serve as a reminder of our pledges. It is a commitment for all time.

Henderson County Earth Day Quilt

New Horizons

wall hanging

III

Teacher

New Horizons: wall hanging

Best Class

Mountain Arts Program

Bringing Coals to Newcastle

A Heartwarming Experience

Words, Words, Words

A Mexican Wedding

Epiphany

Best Class

Tell you
what I liked
Best
about our class

It was oral
poems
readings with
Southern accents

Southerners are
great story-tellers
They savor their
Words
draw them out
roll them around
in their mouths

Listen!

Yummm!

Mountain Arts Program

There is great dissatisfaction with education today. High school dropout rates are soaring. Parents are confused about what is best for their children's education. Teachers are frustrated with the public's distrust in their ability to teach. At the center of all this are the children trying to respond, in many instances, to the demands made on them to achieve unrealistic goals. As a result many lack language, social, and critical thinking skills needed to succeed in the classroom.

Each child comes to school with his/her own cultural and experiential differences. Each comes as a unique individual. They need nurturing, encouragement and respect for where they are coming from. Children don't know what they can't do. They only know what they can do. If they are well guided they will try to do something new to the best of their ability. They need positive experiences to understand. That is one reason why I decided to try to teach the art of quiltmaking to children in the elementary grades in Western North Carolina. They needed to be guided to discover cooperation, responsibility and respect. They need to be allowed to ask questions. They are the ones who will be the future of this country.

Almost one hundred years ago John Dewey, Columbia University Professor of Philosophy told us, "We learn by doing". He said that real experiences are the most meaningful way for helping a child learn. Sylvia Ashton Warner demonstrated this in her book, Teacher. Warner taught Maori children in New Zealand, Aborigines living a tribal life without a written language. They used some iconographic symbols to record important information. Books with words that showed white children living in little white houses in England were being used to teach these children reading. The pictures as well as the words were meaningless to them. Ashton Warner had the children draw pictures and dictate a story. Each child dictated their story to the teacher who then wrote the words under each picture. When each child could read their story, it went home to be read to the family.

Both John Dewey and Sylvia Ashton Warner influenced what I taught and how I taught in my Kindergarten classes. When I taught Kindergarten through sixth grades for the Mountain Arts Program in North Carolina, I used the same approach. The children moved from hands on experiences to documenting with drawings and writing about what they did. I used my experience and knowledge of quilting to weave together a satisfying learning experience for each class. History, elements of visual arts, language arts, math, cooperation, problem solving and how raw materials could be made into a finished product were included. This program was not a template on how to make a quilt with grade school children. It is an example of how meaningful experiences can engage children's minds in learning. After all, learning is a lifetime skill.

Bringing Coals to Newcastle

It was a place set apart from the mainstream. One of those places settled by Scotch/Irish people during the reign of Queen Elizabeth I. These early settlers found safety and security in the 'hollers' and mountainsides of North Carolina. They were safe from unjust laws and taxation. There were no roads connecting them to the outside world. Their way of life remained locked into the language, culture and lifestyle of the Elizabethan period until the twentieth century. During the 1930's depression roads such as the Blue Ridge Parkway and cobblestone schoolhouses were built in places where no roads or schools had existed. Many local people were hired to help. The Civilian Conservation Corps (CCC), composed of young men from the city, came to reforest the mountainsides by planting saplings. The CCC also helped build the cobblestone schools, which stand to this day as a testament to the desire to help make free public education available to all American children.

The Mountain Arts Program assigned me to teach quiltmaking classes in one of these cobblestone schools located in a place called Bee Log. This place did not appear on any of my maps. It was off the beaten track. Roadside signs were rare, so I had to seek help in a small country store to find the road to Bee Log from the highway. The road followed a winding stream. Houses were connected to the road by a bridge that spanned the stream. The blush of spring was evident in the willows along the way. It was difficult to know if the people living in these houses were descendants of the original settlers or some newcomers from outside.

What could I, an outsider, bring to these hardy people who survived living independently here for more than two centuries? They had managed to house, clothe and feed themselves in this wilderness all this time. They came knowing how to create a finished product out of raw materials. They spun wool and cotton to weave into cloth. They sewed clothes from the woven cloth. Scraps from outgrown clothing were pieced together for quilt tops. They made furniture and the cabins they lived in. They made dyes for yarns and cloth from wild plants. Everybody, children and adults, helped. They understood that they had to be neighbors and help each other. Three buildings filled the center of Bee Log: a church, a general store and the cobblestone school set on an acre of ground. There was a ball field and some swings on the playground area. Only the gym and three of the six classrooms were in use. Older children were now bused into the new larger school in town. Nearby in the stream stood a fly fisherman in waders trying his luck.

My schedule was for three days in this school. It usually took me a week to work out my program with each classroom. Much to the children's delight each class had a morning and then an afternoon class with me. I showed them some of my quilts and the tools I used to create them. Each group dictated a vocabulary list about quilts, which was used at the end to write about their experience. Some quilts were made from paper and others from cloth. In the end, each class had made their very own quilt wall hanging. Younger children dictated a chart story using their vocabulary list. Older children each wrote poems, stories, letters or drew pictures. There was creativity and collaboration. They created their own finished product to hang in their classroom for all to see. They understood how to help each other. They experienced how to make a finished product from raw materials. They felt happy and proud of their work.

A Heartwarming Experience

It seems as if the reinforcing activity planned for my literacy class was to be the most dynamic teaching tool this semester. I have been working for a month with three young Mexican women. They have Mexican high school diplomas but are practically non-verbal in English. We have been talking about our families. The students are interested in learning about my family and I am interested in learning about them. We tell about our children and show pictures of brothers, sisters, parents, cousins, aunts and uncles. Knowing one another better bonds us into a trusting group that understands our mutual struggle for English literacy. The students can say things like, "I have a baby", "This is my husband", and "My mother is in Mexico".

It's the day before Valentine's Day. I think it will be fun to make valentines and in the process extend the use of our limited vocabulary. Loving affectionate valentine cards will be created for husbands, or children or parents.

Three students chattering in Spanish tramp into the building. Laden with book bags and knapsacks crammed with books, notebooks and pencils they plop their tired bodies into the rigidity of the metal folding chairs. Their heavy lidded eyes rest on my eager face. They are working women with young children. Their roles as mothers and wives are defined by their culture. Before them on the classroom table are red paper, doilies, glue stick and scissors.

I tell them, "We will make valentines." They respectfully listen to a condensed version of this celebration. My eyes glance over to Estrelita and I see her head resting on her folded arms. I see Dolores' quizzical eyebrows raised to her hairline. Maria's vacant smile sends negative signals to my conscience. To revive them and my self-esteem, I enlist everybody's help in recalling the family vocabulary. They tell me father, mother, baby, sister, husband, daughter which I list on the board. I show them how to fold a rectangle of paper twice so it looks like a store card.

"What would you like to say on your card?" I query. No suggestions or smiles are forthcoming. "You could write Be My Valentine," I offer. There is no flurry of activity. They have to prepare meals, get children to and from day care or school as well as get themselves to and from their ten or twelve hour entry-level factory jobs. They are tired. I'm feeling that this is the silliest most inappropriate activity ever imagined. I start cutting heart shapes from the red paper and use the glue stick and colored pens to demonstrate the potentials of the raw materials. Almost reluctantly they start drawing, pasting and cutting. Dolores has drawn herself and makes the others laugh. Their smiles lubricate an outburst of Spanish chatter. Suddenly the small room is a babble of Spanish and a little English.

"Teacher, how you say, 'Thank you for my children'?"

"How say I love you forever?"

Maria kisses her hand and asks, "How say?"

"Kiss," I say and write it on the board.

Maria glows and writes on her card, "I kiss you baby."

It's working! Slowly they are beginning to speak, read and write English. The ignited activity keeps us over time. Everyone has a valentine to take home to read to his or her loved ones and show how well they are doing in Literacy.

Words, Words, Words

"Teacher, I hear but no understand!" exclaims Dolores. I know she doesn't have a hearing problem. She always responds to my voice with raised eyebrows. The problem for her and my other two students is comprehension. What to do about it? All of them are graduates of Mexican high schools. Their abilities with English language depend on the length of time they've been in the States and the amount of interaction they have had with Americans. Opportunities for them to hear and speak English are limited. They all work at a factory that employs other Latinos. All day they speak Spanish with each other. When Dolores goes home she watches Spanish television shows. Her husband speaks no English. Our twice-weekly classes are the only times she can practice English. Progress is slow. Because these women work ten or even twelve hour shifts. They are already tired when they come to class. They have children to care for. They are lucky that the husbands will sit with the children so they can come to class.

I tell them, "You work so hard. You get so tired. You get burned from the plastic at work. You tell me your supervisor plays favorites with the other girls. Your pay is under the table. Do you think you made a mistake coming here?"

Dolores is quick to tell me, "You think it is fun to cook outside and give yourself a picnic. In Mexico, we can only cook outside. Inside, it makes smoke. We cough and water comes from our eyes. If we want to eat cooked food, we have to cook outside. When it rains, we eat cold food."

Maria says, "There are no Laundromats. We go to the river. We wash clothes with our hands. The water is cold. It comes down from the mountains that have snow on top. Here, on Sunday morning after working a twelve-hour shift for extra pay, we have a big breakfast at MacDonald and go to the Laundromat. Then we sleep all day and night. Then we are ready to go to work Monday morning."

Estralita tells me, "Our houses are small. They have a door and maybe one window. The floors are dirt. No wood, no carpet. Some sleep on mats on the floor. We have wood floors here. Our children are clean." I want them to learn and they want to learn. But for them it can become as Eliza Doolittle sang in My Fair Lady, "Words, words, words. I'm so sick of words....". They read short selections in our current book, The Working Experience. They like the stories. After the first essay, one of them says, "That story is about me." They dictate stories and I type them on my computer. Each student reads her story in class. We now have a list of one hundred sight words they recognize. They can read sentences and paragraphs in our book, but they struggle to speak a complete sentence or paragraph. If they cannot speak, read and write a sentence, they do not own those 100 words. I want to give them ownership of those words. I want them to write, read, speak and comprehend those 100 words.

I take those 100 words to the Literacy office. With the help of the Literacy computer I print three sets of those 100 words on tag board. Each student alphabetizes her set of words, reads them aloud and spells them. I show the students how to make a sentence with them. They take the word cards home to make sentences they will write in their notebooks for the next class. Dolores brings in five phrases like "I happy". They are devoid of verbs.

Estrelita tells me, "I busy. Next time."

Maria brings a list of twenty sentences. They say, "I work", "I read a book," "I have a blue car." She understands how to write a meaningful sentence. The other two see what Maria has done. They are learning how to use nouns, verbs and adjectives in English. The students continue to make new word cards so they can tell me new things. They are determined to read, to write and speak whole sentences. The students are young. They have the future ahead of them. One day they will have word ownership.

A Mexican Wedding

It's Thursday evening and time for our literacy class to meet. My three students' attendance has not been very good for the past month. Maria called during the afternoon saying, "My car…at mechanic. I no…come class. Sorry, Teacher."

Tonight only Dolores has come. She arrives 15 minutes late. The moment I'm ready to leave, she knocks on the door.

"So, Dolores where is your sister, Estralita? She did not call me."

"Teacher, she is what you say una nova. I no say English. You know with un velo."

"You mean first communion? First Communion for her daughter, Veronica? Veronica is about six years old.

"No Veronica. Estralita is wearing velo."

"She's getting married?"

"Yes!"

Now I'm thoroughly confused. Didn't she have three children with the husband she says she loves very much?

"Did they marry in Mexico before coming here?" I ask.

"They marry only signing the book. No Church."

"You mean they had a civil marriage?"

"Yes. Now they have church. You come. Tomorrow night 7:30."

We have a lesson of sorts. You don't bring your phone to church, do you?"

"Okay teacher. But I need to find a very big room for tomorrow".

"It will wait 'til we get out of class."

During the lesson, I can hear the phone murmur in her pocket. She is attentive to our work, but is quick to say good night and be on her way shouting from her car, "Don't forget, Teacher. Tomorrow night 7:30 at Immaculata."

On the way to church, I stop and get a card at the drugstore. I pull into the church parking lot at 7:25 and ask the few Mexican people hanging around outside if this is the right place. It is. I enter the building and then this small grotto like chapel. A young mother and her daughter are seated at one end of a front pew. At the other end of the pew are two women deep in conversation. Are we the wedding guests? Is this wedding on Mexican time? What am I doing here? There is time to look around. I study the prayer book and songbook in the rack in front of me. Everything is in Spanish. The small chapel has graceful ceiling vaults over the elevated altar area. Two small arches flank the large center curve. The two arch supports each display a small indistinguishable holy portrait. Behind the altar are leaded glass windows. Around the sides and back of the chapel hang plaster tiles depicting the Stations of the Cross with English explanations.

Suddenly there is a commotion in the hall. Jumbles of people enter and spill into the pews. The small chapel is crowded with lively men, women, and children. I do not see Dolores. She is the sister of the bride. Where is she?

The young priest enters by the side door and signals to a couple up front to come to the altar. They stand at the altar and write on something. The couple returns to their pew. The priest exits a side door and then appears at center aisle back door. Someone flips a switch and music is heard as the priest slowly walks solemnly towards the altar followed by Estralita and her husband. She is dressed in a long white gown and cradles white lilies and carnations in her arms. Her freshly coiffed hair is crowned with white tulle and flowers. Her husband dressed in a clean white shirt (unbuttoned at the neck) and dark pants walks at her side. They slowly proceed to sit on two chairs facing the altar. As we all sit, there are ear-splitting howls from a small boy. It is Estralita's's youngest. He is scooped up and taken out the back door. A young woman is video taping the wedding and the guests. She aims her camcorder at the altar area and then pans around the assembled.

Fifteen minutes into the ceremony, Dolores shows up with her husband and baby. She sees me and beams. The priest, sotto voce, recites prayers and blessings in Spanish. I catch some of the words but none of the phrases. The word matrimonio is repeated many times. There is standing, sitting, kneeling. The youngest child is back and finds his way to the parents. The bride sits holding him. The two little daughters run up and sit with the parents and then run to sit in the pews with some other children. The children move from pew to pew and sometimes play in front of the altar. This causes the priest to step carefully around them during the ritual. Ignoring the children, the adult relatives quietly follow the order of the ceremony. During communion, the couple that signed the certificate drapes a flowered garland around the shoulders of the bride and groom as if they're tying the proverbial knot.

Another flip of the audio switch and the priest marches down center aisle to rear door followed by the sanctified couple with their children. The wedding ceremony is finished. There is lots of hugging and kissing and a surge of happy chatter. The couple returns to the altar steps for picture taking with various relatives. Dolores is shoving me forward.

"You too teacher." I stand with the couple. There is a flash.

"All these people, family from Florida. You come to party. Come to restaurant."

Outside it is dark. People are getting into cars. Children are laughing and playing with each other.

Dolores comes over and says, "Follow blue van."

The large room at El Paso Restaurant is unable to contain the sounds spewing from giant sized speakers. Men are clustered over to the side. Women and children are sitting at long tables covered with white paper. The bride sits alone at the head table behind a three-tiered wedding cake. Her children carry paper plates piled with macaroni salad and white bread. They sidle onto folding chairs next to their mother. Happy chatter and excitement mingle with the booming speaker sounds. Estralita has her wished for wedding fiesta grande with all her relatives.

It is also a celebration of accomplishment for Dolores, the younger sister. She has managed to organize this celebration. She finds the big room; gets the Florida family to come; and shows what a kind, considerate hostess she is. She meets a challenge and accomplishes her goals.

On the tip of my mind is a simmering hope that I can channel Dolores' and Estralita's new shown capabilities into accomplishing their goal for English literacy. As I leave the festivities, I shout to them over the din of the hubbub, "Don't forget! Come to class on Tuesday. Come at 5:30."

Epiphany

Standing before third graders,
I detect an old woman
spying on me from
the coatroom mirror
Who is she?

Combing my tangled locks,
I behold an old woman
staring back at me
from the looking glass
What does she want?

Striding Main Street
I glimpse an old woman
matching my pace
in storefront windows
Where is she going?

Contemplating still water,
I gaze upon the old woman
reflecting
Who she is
What she wants
Where she's going

It is I

New Horizons 3

wall hanging

IV

The Good Earth

New Horizons 3: wall hanging

New Life

Generations

Sunrise

Bike Ride

Reward / Glitter

Bird / Matins

Harvest / Night Vision

Winter

Winter Solstice

Winter Brews

Spring

April First

A Feast of Daffodils

Weeping Cherry / Drizzle / Pear Tree

Four Seasons: wall hanging

New Life

I arrived in Hendersonville Labor Day weekend, 1986. The only person I knew was a realtor who helped me find a place to rent. One thing I wanted to do was hike and enjoy the outdoors. And there was plenty of it. An article in the newspaper announced that a hiking club was forming and invited interested people to attend a meeting in the park. I went and met Mary Jo Padgett and David Malpass who got us hiking around the countryside. Pretty soon the County Park commissioned us to build a nature trail in the park. It became apparent we could be an agent for the good of the environment in our county. We named our group The Environmental and Conservation Organization (ECO). We had many meetings to make ECO official by writing articles of incorporation and officially registering as a non-profit. We continued to sponsor hikes. But now we could take stands on environmental concerns. One of the first activities was to organize the first countywide Earth Day celebrations. The Earth Day Quilt hangs today in the Community College, and it was my pleasure to design and assemble that quilt. Later on ECO was awarded an Arts Council Grant to have the quilt framed, mounted and installed next to the library at the Community College.

My experiences biking mountain roads and hiking with ECO and the Carolina Mount Club increased my awareness and regard for the frailty of the environment. Many trees on Mount Mitchell, which is the highest peak in the East, stood leafless on the west side. Runoff from golf courses and herbicides were contaminating the pristine mountain waters. Small mansions were being erected on steep mountainsides on unstable soil. Our members got to work. They monitored the purity of water for the County Water Board, protested building in flood plains and promoted recycling. We learned every little effort counts. We learned saving our Good Earth is not for one day; it is for all times.

Generations

We are climbing Mount Pisgah, the one named to honor the biblical Mount Pisgah from which Moses saw the Promised Land. It is in Pisgah National Forest in the Smokey Mountains. It is 5,721 feet above sea level. Our journey is the last 712' of this distance on a stone and rock-strewn path. There is a transmission tower at the summit, which serves western North Carolina. Our climb begins through a rhododendron thicket. A couple of fallen tree giants lie near the trailhead. They are twisted, gnarled and worn to a silver hue.

We pick our way over, around and on stones and rocks. Some of the larger rocks become steps as we begin to ascend. We toil upward as if climbing Jacob's Ladder. "Every rung gets higher, higher". Our breathing becomes shallow and quick and seems to catch in our throats. We stop to rest near an opening in the bare trees. We see tiny buildings and a green sea of mountain ranges in the distance. The sky is clear. We are out of the wind. Ahead blocking the path is a shipwreck hull of a tree trunk blocking the pathway forcing us to walk right or left around it. Coming down a set of stone steps towards us is a small boy followed by his proud parents.

"Did you climb to the top?"

"Oh yes. Now I'm the leader." This is the pleasure of the younger generation.

At turns in the trail, we stop and enjoy the view. Each time buildings in the valley become less distinct and we can see more of the rolling and cresting mountain ranges on the horizon. Steepness increases. More sky becomes visible. We are near the top. Behind us we hear a huffing and a puffing. A running man is coming from behind.

"Why such a hurry this fine day?"

"Because I'm trying to make it up in 20 minutes."

"Why?"

"I'm trying to beat the 25 minutes it took last time."

As he disappears, coming down the steep steps comes a man balancing himself with a pole. I tell him about the 20–25 minute man.

"Oh I did that when I was 40."

"So how old are you now?"

"Seventy-five."

"So am I."

"You don't look it. Where is your white hair?" At that, I doffed my hat to show the glitter of my silver hue.

The straddling legs of the tower come into view and then the viewing platform. We are on top of Mount Pisgah! The swells and undulations of the land beneath rise and dip like an ocean. We are surrounded by a blue sky. Bare deciduous trees and lines of green evergreens bask on distant mountainsides. Overhead, a soaring hawk. How does he feel floating on air currents? Is he out for a joy ride or is he hunting? There are jet trails and new wispy clouds. We sink to the platform floor and feast. We picnic like Pilgrims on nuts, dates, and oranges. A small bird hops about and inspects the far side of the platform for crumbs. We are at the top of the world. We are in our promised land. Other hikers join us. Our brief respite has refreshed us. We ready ourselves for the return. We leave the newest occupants and the bird in possession of the platform. It is time to descend the winding path and the steep stepping-stones. The path plunges and bends as it descends. We round a curve. Approaching us is a young couple. They have a three-month-old baby slung on father's chest. A mountain climber in the making! We are treated to a toothless smile. You are the youngest generation.

The path widens and becomes less steep. We see a woman resting on a fallen log. Her little hound dog is exploring and sniffing the freshly sawed stump.

"How old do you think it is?"

"I can't tell it's age. The saw left too many marks to count the rings. But look at the center of the stump. It's rotted and a colony of insects is at work making new soil. It smells good!"

"Oh yes, regeneration!"

We near the trailhead and are passed by the three hikers who took our places on the mountaintop. They lunge forward with all the vigor and enthusiasm of the young. We pass back through the rhododendron thicket and find a couple of rambunctious girls exploring the ancient silver hued trees. They wonder how old those giant remnants, of a time long gone, might be. There are no rings nor bark to know. Most certainly they are the oldest generation.

This has been a journey through time and space. We have seen what lies along the pathway. We have climbed to the top of the mountain. We have met old and young generations. We have witnessed regenerations. We have seen our Promised Land. Carpemus Diem.

Sunrise

We see
from the plane
at dawn
mountain tops
become islands
in a sea of
morning fog
flowing between
ridges,
to be caught
like snow
in valley crevices

Bike Ride

uphill-downhill
curves loop
wheels hum
gears click

sunlight-shadows
bird song
water sparkles
woodsy smell

graveyard wall
stone seat
road ahead
eternal remain

Reward

On a steep hillside
sheltered in moist woods
two pink ladyslippers

Glitter

Golden shines
yellow dandelions
for yellow butterflies
fleeting pleasures
delightful treasures
of light.

Bird

A bird brown and speckled
a spectator on my fence
A thrush or thrasher perhaps
relocating south, I sense.

It trilled the most enchanting
melody anyone ever did hear
through the long hot summer
promising to return next year

Matins

From sunrise and moonrise
To sunset and moonset
May you have peace
And contentment
In your heart
And mind

Harvest

Cascading acorns,
treasures
squirrels must bury

Night Vision

Stowed like an errant balloon
in the bare branches
of the old maple
a calm moon

Published in Christian Science Monitor, 09/01/2004

Winter

Street lights
outline
tree silhouettes
against
a darkening sky.

A lone bird
sweeps tree tops
seeking sanctuary
above the creek,

reflecting
the sun's last glow
ushering in
a night world.

Winter Solstice

Twas the first day of winter
when my wondering eyes beheld
a lithe cyclist speeding onward
in traffic four stories below

Dressed in red from head to toe
a little red knapsack on her back
Through slush, snow and ice, Mercury
sped around the next turn

I heard her call as she moved from sight,
"Tiz Winter for three months now.
As days get longer, Spring will
arrive around this same corner."

HAPPY SOLSTICE TO ALL!

Winter Brews

Winter blasts into our lives
chilling summer memories

The sun once more, further south
sits lower on the horizon

Blades of grass, cars and roof tops
shimmer in early morning frost

West winds whip leaves from trees
and moan in overhead rafters

Gray clouds roll in and drive
rain hard onto window panes

My husband takes to the kitchen
making stew to warm our spirits

Spring

Steadfast oak leaves
loosed their grip
today
a gentle wind shook their
branches
leaves swooped and
turned
in their ground-ward
descent

all brown and curled
throughout
the winter
they held fast

Now that the Earth is
turning
to spring newness
to the ground they
are cast

April First

Just when I'm beginning
to believe spring has arrived,
a chilly rain comes sweeping
round the east corner,
spattering mud on daffodils,
silencing amorous birds.

April laughs.
I'm tricked again.
I plant mesclum
and wait

A Feast of Daffodils

No heartburn here.

Just feast your eyes on
their succulent beauty.

Savor their boldness
trumpeting spring.

Nourish your soul.

Weeping Cherry

Splattered alongside
gnarled bare branches
dainty pink blossoms

Drizzle

Smokey mists roll
in spring rain
along mountain slopes

Pear Trees

Atop sturdy pear trees
snow white petals shape lacey veils
for young brides of spring

Four Seasons

wall hanging

Sparklers

wall hanging

V

Events

Sparklers: wall hanging

July 4, 2011

Sight Seeing

The Day Before Christmas

Summer Evening Ball Game

Sisterhood

March 21, 2003

Metamorphosis

A Summer Event

Luck

July 4, 2011

A crescent moon hung
above the sunset glow
as the first rockets
bolted upward
to meet the night

faster and faster
light flashes
along the ridge
to the east, to the west
now back and forth
higher and higher
sparkles, clusters
circles of light
exploding all around
the sky is on fire

hail to
freedom
liberty
justice
for all

Sight Seeing

A street fair is an explosion of merriment
a parade of hellos from other pedestrians,
sociable invitations for front porch visits.
No one is a stranger tonight.

A blended chorus of happy talk and laughter,
how about a drink, wine, beer, tea
or a free hug from a young man with long arms,
promises of hot corn from drifting grill smoke
sweet-tartness of frozen lemon ice
sidewalk bean bag games,
come on and have a throw.

Neighborly revelry abounds
music weaves through the crowd
jazz under the tent, blues on the corner
old and young beating and pounding
on a congregation of drums
a storehouse of glowing memories to save
for arctic winter weather, arriving too soon.

The Day Before Christmas

'Twas the day before Christmas
and I'd paid the bill
So what is this wondrous,
God awful chill?
Temperature's dropping
Where is the heat?
My wandering eyes beheld
no flicker, nor flame
to warm cold feet.
Quick as a wink
I sprang to the phone
to call Public Service
about this matter.
Right away there was
an answer tone
A friendly voice
replied all chatter
to my cry for help
on this cold, cold night,
"For one and all this
is winter vacation
You must wait I fear
four days.
We want to play.
We will remedy
your situation
by next Tuesday."
So we put on our
scarves, hats and boots
Took shovel, ski and sleigh
and frolicked
until New Years Day

Summer Evening Ball Game

Hur-rah
the game begins
a crack of the bat
double play
cheers

Waitresses running
nachos, foaming beer
to front box seats
joyful fans

Dropped ball
missed plays
stolen bases
groan

In the restroom
girls primp and chatter
in passageways
boys swagger

As the sun sets
horrible fumbles
losing big time
restless children

The sky darkens
floodlights shine
another game
tomorrow night

Sisterhood

I follow you
you follow me
I walk in your footsteps
You walk in mine
Round and round
we circle

A sisterhood in black
We flock together
In Madrid
In New York
In Buenos Aires
In Toronto
In Rome
Silently asking,
stop violence
to have peace

Our footsteps
sigh
How long?
Will we learn?

We are tall
We are short
We are old
We are young
Mujeres de Negro
Para la Paz

We are experienced
We are patient
We are dedicated
We want to stop violence
We want to have peace
from Bethlehem
To Belfast
To Baghdad
To Belgrade
To Beijing
I walk in your footsteps
You walk in mine

March 21, 2003

The awe and wonder of spring
arrives to equal light and dark
The earth rotates to renewal
'midst flourishing weeds of fear

The awe and wonder of spring
brings heavy downpours in Baghdad
where planes plant bombs for a harvest
of smoke plumes and fire blossoms

In awe and wonder a TV
war announcer delivers scores
of battle wins and losses,
a father displays a picture,
"Mr. Bush, you took my only son"

In awe and wonder arrives
creation and destruction
American weapons demolish
the Cradle of Civilization.

Metamorphosis

The intersection of their lives
happened near the autumnal equinox
she walked in the balm of sun
he drove under clear blue skies
they met at the corner

Taking care she stepped into the road
half-way across green turned
yellow
she increased her pace

At yellow caution
he turned left
saw her red hat
too late

Steel smashed flesh and bone
flung her up on car hood
down on hard ground
like discarded trash

She screamed
Sirens wailed
witnesses fled the spectacle
"I didn't see her," he whined

A Summer Event

I stop by the birdseed store to use a gift certificate. When I park the car, I see these finches fluttering around and perching all over a feeder at the edge of the parking lot. So I get the same kind of feed, a bag of sunflower chips. I want to see finches at my feeder, too.

Later, I hang the feeder containing this newest seed offering off the deck railing. Soon excited Goldfinches, Purple Finches, and House Finches are feeding. On Sunday morning, I'm sitting on the deck talking on the phone with a friend and along comes a Bluebird family; Mom, Pop, and Baby. The father positions himself on one of the highest perches. Baby gets on one of the low perches, and Mom's watching on the sidelines. Pop starts eating seeds. He takes one for himself and then pops one in Baby's mouth. Baby, stretching his neck to reach up for Dad's gifts, keeps chirping and gulping seeds as fast as they're served. When Mom notices me, she starts fluttering and chattering. Pop continues eating and feeding Baby. This is too much for Mom. She grabs one of Baby's legs and pulls him off the perch. This causes him to lose his balance and land on the edge of one of the planters. That doesn't discourage the father. He just flutters down from the perch to poke a seed in Baby's open mouth and goes back up for his share and the next seed for Baby. Mom is getting agitated. She scolds the kid and her mate. Placidly, they continue the eating/feeding routine. Beside herself with angst, she hears my voice and notes my 'huge' presence. Finally Mom has had enough. She grabs Baby's leg so he has to loosen his grip on the planter. He flutters and flies off with Mom to the big tree. Pop gorges a few more of the seeds and reluctantly follows, joining their westward flight.

Amazing to witness such distinct male and female characteristics in tiny creatures! Mom is protecting her young. Pop is willing to risk. The baby is completely innocent of any problems. His mission is to eat.

Published Christian Science Monitor, September 1, 2003

Luck

For every lucky lottery winner there are hundreds, maybe thousands of losers. I seldom win anything of monetary value; so rarely buy tickets of chance. Oh, I did win five Susan B. Anthony silver dollars at a concert one time. On the other hand my husband seems to buy a winning ticket almost every time he gets one. He's come home with bottles of wine, or a turkey, or a share of a winning lottery ticket. Perhaps I don't know all the contests he enters; but when he enters he smiles and says he knows his ticket is a winner.

One time when we were eating breakfast with friends they tell us about their visit to the Indian casino resort the previous night. She can't say enough about the luxurious furnishings and decorations in the new hotel. She tells us, "There are these gorgeous chairs. You sink down and tilt back in them; and the food, all premium stuff, no dinners under twenty dollars. Guess what it costs for the best steak dinner?" Before we can say anything, she tells us, "Ninety-nine dollars. We weren't up for that so we ate in the casino's Chinese restaurant. No extra charge for rice or tea and we got all the shrimp we ever wanted!"

When she slows down her monologue, he says, "There's lots of smoking in the place. The gamblers all smoke and there's clouds of smoke in the restaurant. Besides that the ones who can least afford it are gambling." On the way home from breakfast we pass a bus that's flashing a sign saying 'OZONE ALERT' instead of the route name and number. Polluted air abounds in the casino and on the road.

That evening we're at a park band concert. My husband plays trombone with the featured jazz group. I'm sitting in the shelter knitting to exercise my arthritic fingers while the band sets up. A woman perches herself next to me on the bench. She asks what I'm making and I tell her. She says "If I'd known you were going to be here I would have brought you a couple of skeins of yarn I found in the apartment after my mother died." A generous thought from a woman I've never met before.

Two men are circulating in the audience selling tickets for a 50/50 raffle. I pull out my wallet. You can buy three tickets for two dollars or an arm's length of tickets for five dollars. The money goes into a fund that pays for next year's concerts. I tell them to come back just before drawing so my ticket might be on top of the pile and maybe I'd win. The woman who has her mother's yarn says, "Before I came tonight, I counted what money was left from my Social Security. There was six dollars and it's a week until the month ends. So I decided not to bring money tonight."

The drawing is at intermission. There's a flurry of ticket buying just before the drawing my husband buys an arm's length and gives it to me. I buy three tickets. A member of the audience is chosen to draw the winning ticket number. Sure enough it's one of Fran's number. The ticket man hands me a roll of bills (half of the night's collection).

During the second half of the concert, I think about the woman who has only $6 and how much more than that amount is in my pocket now. I don't think she'll go hungry in this close-knit community. At the same time, I want to enjoy the winning with my husband who plays in the band. We don't need to do anything grand like a $99 steak dinner to enjoy this little windfall.

Before we leave, I go over to the raffle men and give them back half of the wining money so that the woman and her friends can come to the park next year to have the pleasure of a concert on a summer's evening. Isn't there a saying that one cannot live by bread alone?

©2007

Log Cabin/House Variation

wall hanging

VI

Family

Log Cabin/House Variation: wall hanging

The Old Samovar

My gaze upon a
bouquet of coreopsis,
daisies and roses
set in the old samovar.

A pastel portrait created
long ago.
Mother's hands deftly
stroking chalks on paper.

The gleaming samovar
that forever sat atop
the radiator cover
in our dining room.

The garden where
flowers bloomed
guided by
Father's hands.

Those are my
good memories
Those are my
peaceful memories.

Published in Freeing Jonah IV

Family Reunion

Blown here
by winds of opportunity
our forebears
built new lives
from old

Like milkweed
taking root
descendants scattered
to cultivate their lives

Returning briefly
we flock together
in the kindness of kinship
sharing new histories
and old memories

Hearts and minds reconnect
familial bonds link
uniting generations
growing new lives from old.

Tradition

'Twas a Thanksgiving to remember
despite the snows of November.

Here was the sharing of our food
that brightened our wintry mood.

A turkey browned to perfection
arrived via Susan's[1] able direction.

Beans yams and whipped potatoes
kept miss Laura[2] on her dancing toes.

Sweet and delicious were the tarts
presented by Eric[3] to warm our hearts.

We ate and ate with all our might
'til no one had any appetite.

Whew! What an awful mess to
cleanup without distress.

Then Ranger Rob[4] and Mr. Jackson[5]
carried out fantastic cleanup action.

To all it was a time to remember
This wintry day in November.

© 2000

[1] *Daughter*
[2] *Granddaughter*
[3] *Grandson*
[4] *Son-in-law*
[5] *Dog*

A Short Life

When I come home from work, I find him looking as dead as any being could possibly appear. This isn't the first time he had been found lying at the bottom of his cage. Not an eyelid flutters. In fact, the gray lids covering his eyes indicate what I fearfully suspect: our pet canary, Frank Sinatra is dead.

He started falling off his perch a few months before. This upsets the girls so much that they insist on taking him to the veterinarian. We all stand around the examining table while the vet gently inspects Frankie.

"This bird has something I can't do anything about," he says. "He has a brain tumor, and we don't do brain surgery on canaries."

I think back to that morning, when our newspaper delivered an offer we can't resist: an ad for a canary with a cage, stand included. That afternoon, we go to Woolworth's after the girls finish with school. In the back of the store, next to the escalator, is the pet department. The escalator carries shoppers to a mezzanine that has a lofty ceiling. An open, spacious expanse, it must be four stories above street level. We tell the saleslady we have come for the special canary offer. From under the counter she takes a little box with holes in it and a small net with a long handle. She leads us to an enormous cage where a great number of birds are flitting about and chirping. They are all shades of yellow and look like the hungry goldfinches that come to our birdfeeder in the winter.

"Choose the one you want and I'll catch it for you," the sales lady says.

The girls watch the birds and find one they both like. Slowly, the saleslady slides the net between the cage bars and snags the bird, guiding the bird to the cage door where her other hand holds the box. She slides the door open. Out comes the bird, not into the box. It flies up, up, up towards the far distance ceiling. The fleeing bird joins a flock of other escaped birds migrating to the four corners of the high ceiling. As the canary flies up, the corners of the girls' mouths droop down.

"Don't worry, girls. Just choose another canary and I'll get it for you," the saleslady tells them.

Reluctantly, they watch the other birds hopping around in the big cage and eventually find one they think is almost as good. This time the saleslady boxes the bird. We bring our new pet home with cage, stand, and food. We name him after Frank Sinatra because he is known as a "canary" for his singing. The girls hope to hear long, melodious songs from Frankie. My hope is that it will sing like that bird we had when I was a child. It sang and sang for hours on end, and he liked to sing along with music on the radio. In the summer, my mother hung the cage in the yard, so our canary would be inspired to sing more when it heard the wild birds. One summer, the cage door mysteriously sprang open, and the canary flew off. We never heard from it again.

When Frankie Sinatra's short life ends, we decide to have the best funeral possible. One girl digs a hole under the lilac bush. We place him in a small box lined with the softest tissue possible. Gently, we lay the closed box in the hole and cover it with dirt. The other girl plays her flute practice piece, the only song she knows.

I don't recall Frankie Sinatra singing at all. But the girls insist he did. It was the finding, getting and having our own pet that meant the most. Losing him was a hard lesson about life. Nothing lasts forever except memories. And so he remains one of our most vivid family stories.

Juice in Her Battery

"Nobody lives forever," she said flatly.

"That's such an abstract, clinical statement," I shoot back over the phone. I'm talking with my 80-year old sister, Jo, who's been dealing with leukemia for about 10 years. Most of that time she's been in remission and she's made it her business to explore every corner of the earth she wants to visit. Her husband, Charlie is a homebody and prefers to stay behind puttering around the house, playing golf, and drinking coffee with his buddies. He says that it's too hard keeping up with her. Last year she persuaded him, my husband and I to go on a tour to Spain. She especially wanted to visit Africa and there was an optional overnight to Morocco. She got there. Charlie did enjoy it and bought a rug for their house.

She's visited the Galapagos two times. She's gone as far south as Tierra del Fuego and plans to visit Alaska this summer. A couple of years ago she flew to New Zealand because her son was working there and it was such a good opportunity. She persuaded our brother, Arthur, to go with her. They toured North and South Islands and she found a tour guide to take her on a nature trail she read about in the New York Times. It was such an exceptional experience that she was considering a second trip out there when we were flying back from Spain.

Her love is the outdoors. She's climbed mountains in the Rockies, the Cascades, the Teton Range, Smokies, and the Adirondacks. In the winter she loves cross-country skiing. She's a botanist and Audubon member with a life list of birds she has seen at home and in her travels.

For her seventieth birthday, she invited the family to celebrate with her at a country inn in the Catskills. During that week end, she led us up a steep, stony mountain trail. As she forged ahead, she called back over her shoulder, "Don't feel you have to keep up with me. Do rest if you need to. I'll wait up ahead for you."

In between her mastectomies and before we knew about this other cancer, we got a $300 special fare, round trip tickets to Frankfort, Germany. Part of that trip was a visit to our paternal grandfather's hometown, Arad, Romania. It was shortly after the Ceausescu regime had been overthrown and the Balkan strife eruption. It turned into quite an adventure

This past winter her white cell count went up and her red cell count went down. She went back on oral chemo. After the third round of chemo the count is back to normal and the platelets are holding. She's focused on Alaska. The itinerary is set. The tickets are bought. She's got something going every day. Charlie's not the only one who can't keep up with her. None of us can. No matter, she'll wait up for us.

Springing into Summer

Winter is gone. The piles of gray tired snow have left, replaced with green lawns; trees crowned with various shades of green; rainbows of flowers blooming in yards, lawns, curb barriers and parks. Highland Park has made us dizzy with lilac perfume, magnificent magnolias, dinner plate size tree peony flowers. Abundant rains to last a lifetime have soaked the roots of every plant.

We celebrate everyday, everywhere the beauty we behold and the return of warm sun. People flock to the parks, eat outside, bicycle and relax on benches and lawns. First we had the lilac festival. Coming up is the jazz festival on the street and in various indoor venues. The park department sponsors many guided hikes, bike rides, canoe & kayak river tours until October first. Landmark Society offers guided walks throughout the city. City Market has started up with fresh local vegetables. Right now, the plant growers are selling colorful flats of perennials and a few local farmers have eggs, asparagus and rhubarb. When the season gets started up to 40,000 people attend.

Our family has celebrated all birthdays this past month. Rob and I are the bookends. He celebrates at the end of April. In between we party with Fran, then Susan, followed by Bel and ending with me. Lots of good food, smiles and cheer all around!

I did not rejoin the book group this semester but haven't stopped reading. I just finished reading The River of Doubt. It's about Teddy Roosevelt's last exploration, which takes place in South America. Roosevelt takes along his son Kermit and they travel to the center of Brazil to descend an unmapped river. The unexpected challenges they met engrossed me completely. I'm currently reading Wicked: the Life and Times of the Wicked Witch of the West by Gregory Maguire. Yes, it relates to the Oz stories. The author imagines the origins of the Witch of the West and her relationship with Glenda. It's on the surreal side except for human nature and human values. Need I say more?

Love getting all your notes and letters. Keep the connection.

Cheers and love, Carla

A Visit to Our Romanian Cousin*

It was a cold, overcast December day when my sister, Jo and brother-in-law, Charlie and I arrived at the Keleti train station in Budapest. The Balkans were seething with unrest and we were close to their borders. In 1989 the Romanian Dictator Ceausescu had been deposed and assassinated. It was a very unsettled region of the world. Our destination was Arad, Romania, the city from whence our paternal grandfather emigrated to America in the late 1800's. Arad was part of Hungary until after World War I when it was annexed to Romania. We wanted to meet our cousin, Margareta Braun who had survived the Nazi invasion during World War II and Russian occupation after that war.

We found our first class seats in a dirty, rickety coach and bought sandwiches and bottled water from vendors hawking their wares out on the platform. The train was called The Orient Express which had conjured up for us visions of movie grandeur. There was no dining car or any comforts. It was a good thing we did buy food. Our trip became a grueling six-hour journey on poorly maintained tracks traveling over a vast snow covered plain under gray skies: a frosty-looking land stretching to the horizon. Occasionally we saw a shepherd, crook in hand, tending his flock or gleaners pulling ears of corn from dry stalks. Horse drawn wagons replaced trucks. It felt as if we had traveled back in time.

Arad lies just 17 kilometers from the Romanian boarder and was reached not long after going through customs. On the outskirts of the city, we saw factory buildings with broken windows, rusting storage tanks, and machinery. The train pulled in front of a large, grimy station. We stepped out onto the platform where many people milled about. Inside, women in shawls, long dresses, and aprons were sweeping with twig brooms. Outside, throngs of people and enterprising hawkers were selling digital watches, socks and cigarettes. Charlie found a taxi driver who spoke English. First he brought us to the bank to exchange money. He drove carefully, dodging potholes, past the WWII monument honoring slain Russian soldiers. We passed the large, once grand concert hall that hinted there had been better times. In 1989 the Romanian people had revolted against their dictator Nicolae Ceausecu who had bankrupted the country and subjected them to constant surveillance, He had been a brutal ruler since 1965. Now they were trying to establish their country as a Republic.

At the bank, we found lines of people trying to exchange their Lei for "hard" currency. According to the taxi driver, gasoline prices had gone from 50 Lei to 150 Lei in just one day. We received 270 Lei for each dollar exchanged. The largest banknote was a 100 Lei bill. It was impossible to stuff the newly acquired paper money into my wallet. One overnight stay including breakfast the next morning cost 9,000 Lei ($34) at the Parc Hotel. Indeed the country was still struggling.

After storing our belongings in our hotel rooms, we set out to find our cousin. We walked past dirty, cracked buildings and crumbling courtyard walls. Shops were dimly lit with little or nothing on display. People in the street were dressed in dark, drab clothing. No cheerful chatter could be heard. With the help of some locals, we managed to find the house and then the door of our elderly relative.

Petite and vivacious, the 85-year old Margareta Braun greeted us in English and welcomed us into her one-room apartment, which was part of a large building that had been subdivided into several apartments. After passing back and forth to bring us tea and food, she recounted family history and related anecdotes about our grandfather who had died before I was born. It was he who had taught her the words to "Yankee Doodle" when she was very young. She told us our family had been merchants living in comfortable circumstances. The family home was a large Victorian structure near the river. Under the Communists, all private property was confiscated by the state, so she had to give up her home and move into a one-bedroom apartment. It is where she has had to live for 50 years. She stuffed everything she could into her apartment: a grand piano, cluttered bookcases, family heirlooms, credenzas, clocks, a large portrait of a young Margareta, tables, and chairs, and a bed. Old photos, letters and mementos were collected in boxes and drawers.

In one corner, a small ceramic tile stove stood. It was the only source of heat in the room. It was warm if you sat near it, cold when at any distance. Despite her cramped and cold quarters, Margareta cherished her independence and enjoyed having a "home" of her own. We learned that she spoke English, Romanian, Hungarian and German, and that she taught German to the young people who were interested in emigrating. She used songs, games and stories to enrich her instruction. Once a day, a hot meal was delivered to her by local Social Service. She had a full and active life for a woman of her age. Before we left, she presented us with a diagram of the cemetery where our ancestors rest. But best of all a skillfully constructed family tree that went back generations to our shared heritage. What a prize! Here were the roots and the tree: a gift that we, and our descendants, will treasure. How had she managed to survive the atrocities of WWII I wondered?

"Well," she said, "the Germans saved me." That was stunning news after I had learned about Nazi brutality! It seems that the Romanian peasants had rounded up all the Jews and planned to kill them, but before they could carry out this murderous plan, the Germans arrived and released the Jews. It was fortunate for Margareta, but her husband was taken to slave labor which he did not survive.

Despite her difficult life, Margareta has lived with dignity and spirit. She pins her hopes for the future on her aspiring students. The memory of her and how she has triumphed is a legacy I will always cherish.

*Published, The American Jewish Outlook, April 1992

Triptych

window quilt

VII

Portraits

Triptych: window quilt

Impressions

The Come Back Kid

A Song in His Heart

Cinderella

Coming Clean

Mule Man

Appalachian Trails #2 ½: wall hanging

Impressions

Is there somebody or some experience that has made a great impression on you or influenced your life? Right away I think of my Aunt Mim, our mother's older sister who lived to be 100. She was a career woman, traveled extensively and never married until she was sixty. Born in 1883 into a world that expected a woman to serve men and nurture children, she trained to be a kindergarten teacher and attended Columbia University to be a librarian. She worked at the Hebrew Orphan Asylum (HOA) on Amsterdam Avenue in New York, first, as a counselor in the boys dormitory and then as the HOA librarian. She traveled extensively, visiting France twice before WWII. She owned a car and drove across the U.S. with a friend and Grandma. Another time she went on a pack train trip in the Rockies. She loved the outdoors and took us hiking, camping and ice-skating. We learned to adventure and that we could be and do anything if we chose to work at it and make it happen.

World War II began during my first year of high school. It was a time of fighting tyranny and fear. By the time I graduated we had peace when I went off to college to learn to be a teacher. It was a new world with possibilities. I met May Kedney who taught Freshman Art Appreciation. She was also the adviser to our Outing Club. One time she chaperoned us on an overnight bicycle trip to a farm where we slept on hay in a barn and cooked our meals over an open fire. She advised us; "Keep the faculty of effort trained", "You have to expect the unexpected", "Chance favors those who are prepared". Good advice not only for teaching but for life.

About twenty years after I graduated college I met May again as a colleague teaching art in the same school where I taught first grade. She was an inspiring teacher. Her presentation of the materials and theme for the children's art class activity made those young students impatient to get their hands working. When I taught in the Mountain Arts program I prepared for, introduced lessons and gave instruction as she had done. I was delighted to have the students and their teacher satisfied and happy with what was created.

Later on when I was making and teaching patchwork, I asked her to show me how to use over the counter fabric to make my quilt designs more vibrant. Years before she had worked one summer with Josef Albers on his Homage To The Square book. She invited me to her studio apartment for a weekend. "Bring your cloth scraps with you," she directed. We made color wheels and color value charts and some Albers' squares with the scraps. We worked on value, harmony, texture, shade and composition. For me, this became a new language of seeing.

The Come Back Kid

"They're calling me the 'come back kid' now," he says. A smirk brightens his gaunt face as he leans back in the lounge chair. His bony frame sinks into the cushions. This is Stanley's third trip to Hospice House. The first time he stayed long enough to let them know he really didn't belong there. He called a taxi and came back home. He's been my neighbor almost five years. We inhabit an older apartment building where walls are shared. Not too unlike a family in a private home, it provides a special kind of intimacy. One has to learn others' shortcomings and habits.

Stan came from New York and let us know quickly his peeves and needs. He had been disabled on the job earlier in his life and was put on compensation. Oh, he had some good times before the accident. Traveled a bit but never settled for family life. His injury at times was a torment. He complained that I should be quieter because he didn't sleep well at night. *"Your feet clatter on the stairs," he said. "Why are you so noisy in the kitchen?" "Don't slam the front door."* Nothing seemed to please him. He was sarcastic and caustic and had few friends. But when he had a good night and there was no pain, he joked and told anecdotes when we met in the hall or in front of the building.

The second time he went to Hospice was by van. One of our downstairs neighbors heard him fall and phoned up to see if my husband, Fran could look in on him. By this time Stan was leaving the apartment door unlocked so that the Hospice workers could check on him. Fran found him conscious with a small cut on his head and struggling to stand. That afternoon at Hospice, Fran looked in on Stan and discovered him comfortably unconscious. We thought this was it and hurried over to see him the next morning. Much to our surprise there was Stan sitting up in bed, eating and preparing to get back to his apartment.

When Fran practices his trombone he plays 40's jazz. Also he's a patient listener. Both of these talents Stan appreciated. They brought some contentment into his life. After Stan returned from Hospice the second time, Fran went over for a short visit. Stan took that opportunity to ask Frank to take him to a particular car dealer. He wanted to trade in his old gas guzzling van for a newer model. My husband agreed to help. I was furious. "Why are you enabling him to carry out this futile acquisition?," I hissed.

"Because that's what he wants to do and I understand it."

It took a couple of visits to the car dealer to make the trade. Stan's spirits seemed to improve as negotiations moved along. Fran came home saying, "I learned a lot about bargaining. Stan sure knows how to maneuver a deal despite the shape he's in." It wasn't long before the newer car was parked out front. Maybe Stan drove it about ten miles altogether before he went back to Hospice the last time. For about two weeks he lingered drifting further from our shores. The nurses marveled at how tenaciously he held on to that slender thread of life. Perhaps he died satisfied with how well he managed to make a deal. Maybe it provided a short lease on a few more days among the living.

There was no memorial service. Only a very few living here knew him. I think about the Jewish prayer for the dead. It tells us that we live on in the minds and hearts of those who knew us. And so he does.

A Song in His Heart

It was a happenstance that was as graceful as a movement on the dance floor. There we were sunning ourselves this early fall day. We each sat on either end of a low stone wall that separated a municipal parking lot and a Main Street sidewalk. Nearby college students were socializing. A couple of them were playing instruments like a guitar and an ocarina. Their chatter and musical notes drifted over us. People leisurely strolled past. The perception that financial institutions were suffering and failing somewhere beyond this place wasn't apparent. It was a tranquil scene. He folded the newspaper he had been reading, slowly rotated his body, regarded me and said, "Nice day". I agreed it was.

"Where you from?"

"Hendersonville."

"I've lived here all my life, you know. I'm a dancer."

"What kind of dancing?"

"I do clogging. I danced at the college, too. I danced with The Sunshine String Band out of Charlotte. There's one guy from Oklahoma, a guy from Raleigh, and this girl from Charlotte. Boy can she sing and play the fiddle, too. All three of them play banjo and I dance with them. We performed in the stadium. There were 1700 people there to see Taj Mahal. What a crowd! We were the head liners for Taj Mahal. Can you believe that? Not ever in my dreams had I thought about such a thing. I danced with another banjo band, too. They were three white boys from Cornell. They're very good, but the ones from Charlotte they know how to play. I don't want people to believe Hip Hop is black music. We do better than that. We let people see how good black music can be. Most of the people there were white and they loved what we did. People get the wrong idea about black performers. I've been written up in a couple of magazines, you know."

"How did you learn to dance?"

"I just watched people doin' it. And I kept practicing every chance I got. It just comes naturally to me now."

"Can you really support yourself clogging with the Sunshine Band?"

"Not really. I dance for free because I see how much people like it. One time this woman brought her grandchildren to see me dance. They loved it. So the grandmother had taps put on their shoes. Now when they're with her they practice the dancing they learned from watching me. I'm so proud I could start those kids dancing. They're white, you know."

"But that doesn't keep a roof over your head or food on the table"

"I know. I have a truck and help people move. But things are slow now. Everything's tight for everyone. People are staying where they're at. Times are gonna get better, soon I hope. I'm forty-seven years old. My Mama told me never put anyone down. That's not right. I don't ever put anyone down. I had a roommate who kept putting me down. I kicked her out. I won't ever put anyone down and I won't have anyone put me down."

In the end I felt I had a waltz with a man of principle. A man rich with a memory of performing in front of all those white people. Letting them know how good black music can be.

Cinderella

I was standing behind them in the checkout line at K-Mart; mother, father and two quietly patient girls. Each of the girls had a costume draped over one thin arm. Clutched in the other arm was a large slender book. The taller girl may have been about nine or ten years old. The smaller girl looked to be about five or six. The mother leaned over and whispered something to the father and left. As the trio reached the counter, the bigger girl handed her costume and book up to the father, who placed them on the counter. Then the smaller girl handed up her unwieldy load. Instead of her total costume being on the hangar, a small packet containing a wig had slipped off the hanger.

"You messed with this, didn't you," he snarled.

"No, that's the way Mommy put it on my arm," she murmured.

"I don't think so. We'll see who's telling the truth when we see Mommy."

During this exchange, the bigger girl did not speak. She gazed into space keeping a blank expression. There was no further comment or conversation between or among them. The three left the store, as my purchases were tabulated.

Outside ahead of me, walking together in the parking lot was the family of four. The bigger girl, skipping along between both parents, held hands with them. Nobody held the smaller girl's hand as she shuffled along behind the trio. No one spoke.

Coming Clean

I stumble into the laundry room with loaded basket. It's Saturday morning, a favorite time to get chores done. Machines are churning, humming and whirling. Two other tenants are tending their loads of wash. She's loading a washer. He's unloading a dryer.

She says," Whatever happened to that stray we all fed?"

An upturned lid beckons me to an empty machine.

He replies, "They hadta put him away. Couldn't be trained nohow." He's pulling his dry jeans out and laying them on the table. "It's like that woman I knowed. She was abused as a child. They told her if she married, never to have chillen. She'd most likely abuse them. She couldn't help herself. Ya know. Well that dog was abused. He'd never be good around people. Ya know".

He's medium height with a swelling paunch. He's wearing shoes and no socks. I speculate to myself, "Are all his socks dirty or is this a current fashion statement?"

He continues, "Jes' like my former wife. She played around behind' my back. Wants those monthly payments zactly on time. A day late and she's after the money." He's smoothing his jeans on the table. Short strong fingers caress the wrinkles. The legs are matched. Jeans are are folded and next pair are laid on the table. "Got my boy through cooking school. He's a chef. Girl's in high school. If they needs something, I get it for them. Their cars break down, I fix 'em. Cook' em a steak on my grill when they come over."

She asks, "How long since you been divorced?"

"Seven years" is the reply.

Mule Man

He's talking on the phone when we enter the Bureau of Land Management Visitors Center in Cannonville, Utah. He tips and swivels his long, lean frame in the office chair as he speaks emphatically into the mouthpiece. His cowboy hat is tilted back on his head. Nearby the ranger sits behind the counter doing some sort of paper work. It's April 30th. We are on our way from snowy Bryce Canyon National Park to Capitol Reef National Park. We will be driving through the Escalante on our way and want to know if it's worthwhile to take the time to visit Kodachrome Basin State Park which is up the same road as this visitors center.

The ranger comes over to where we are attempting to get our bearings on a large relief map depicting the 1.9 million acres of the Grand Staircase-Escalante Monument located in the Colorado Plateau in south-central Utah. It is an area of red rock canyons and high plateaus containing millions of years of geological earth history. The ranger points out specific landmarks we will pass and suggests a couple of short hikes.

"The features of Kodachrome Basin are similar to the Escalante," he tells us. "It might take more time than you have." We regretfully agree because we are only half way along our planned itinerary.

The man is finished with his phone conversation and strides over to us. He asks if we are going to Kodachrome Basin.

"We don't think so."

"I was hoping to get a ride up that way. Got a mule camp 'bout three miles out."

"That's no bother. Glad to drive you out."

He settles into the car's backseat. He tells us he's camping with his three mules. He's from Sun Valley, Idaho on an off-road journey to Creston, B.C. from the south rim of the Grand Canyon. His name is Jake. He spent four years planning this journey using maps and GPS. One year he drove the route marking his campsites and making arrangements for mule food drops. He feeds the mules compressed fodder pellets and was running low at the present site. He was contacting the supplier when we met.

"Want to see my camp-site and the mules?"

"Of course!"

After parking the car, we clamber down the roadside embankment. Sheltered by the sandy bank is a small blue tent. Nearby carefully set on the ground are two white wooden boxes. "I made these boxes. They're my kitchen. They hold my cooking equipment and supplies. They form a table when I set them up to prepare a meal and eat." Nearby two mules are tethered with stout ropes. The third mule clanging a cowbell on its neck comes plodding over to us and nuzzles Jake. "These animals are bonded. As long as one or two are tethered, the loose one won't wander far. This one's Bernie. He carries the kitchen." He scratches the neck of the first tethered mule. "This one carries the equipment, and I ride this other one."

"Why did you choose to ride mule?"

"I made furniture until I injured my back. I started riding mule after I had a spinal fusion a few years ago. Riding is supposed to be good for my back."

"When did you start this trip?"

"We started out on April 17 going down the south side of the Grand Canyon. There were a lot of folks descending with big packs on their backs. It wasn't possible to pass them. We crossed the Colorado by bridge and ascended to the north rim. This segment has taken me more time than I planned. I've decided that I won't be disappointed if I can't get it all done in the projected seven months."

The look in his eyes shows hopeful resolve. He's come through some rough wilderness to get this far and knows he will encounter more of the same. It's a lonely, challenging adventure that he and those faithful mules undertake. We think of him every day out there adventuring north through sun and rain, heat and cold, and back pain. He is the spirit of exploration in this mechanically driven world. He has the pioneer daring of the explorer adventuring into the unknown challenging his stamina. It's gratifying to meet someone who has the plucky courage to try to make his dream come true. When we part we shake hands and wish one another safe journey.

Appalachian Trails #2 ½

wall hanging

Appalachian Trails #2

wall hanging

VIII

Travel

Appalachian Trails #2: wall hanging

Our First Car

Tracking Seminole Patchwork

Say No to Pollution Letter

Canajoharie

December 1995 Letter

Touring New York State Canal

The Promised Land

Our First Car

Fran has dearly treasured being able to study and learn. He researches most of the time to make educated decisions and rarely takes risks, but there was that one time when he bought our first car. It was a coupe with a rumble seat. The fact that the floorboard was missing on the passenger side didn't matter that much. The price was right, so we got it. I didn't drive in those days, so I always sat straddling the floor opening watching the road slide beneath us as we 'roared' along at up to 25 mph. Every 50 miles or so Fran had to feed the engine a quart of oil. It probably burned more oil than gas. Gas was about 25 cents a gallon in 1950 and no doubt cheaper than oil. This particular kind of car got started by putting a crank into a special opening in the front and turning it quickly and hard to make the engine turn over: a feat not easily accomplished by a 100-pound woman.

One time we had to go to Albany, which was about 65 miles away. We loaded four quarts of oil in the back and sped off on our longest trip. We stopped outside of Albany to check the oil dipstick and pour in one of the spare quarts of oil. It was essential to just keep the motor running once the car was started.

Some of Albany's streets were paved with slippery cobblestones. When we got on those cobblestones, the car shimmied wildly even at 5 mph. At an intersection, the traffic light turned red and when we stopped. So did the motor.

Fran climbed out, ordered me to sit behind the wheel with one foot on the brake and the other foot ready to gently depress the gas pedal when the crank turned the engine over. By the time we had the engine running again there were crowds on all four corners gaping and cheering as we chugged through the intersection. We made it back home the same day and didn't stall again.

Not long after our visit to Albany, the car died at the curb in front of our house. It just wouldn't start. Fran tried selling it, but no buyers felt the challenge to have it. Finally, he called a junk dealer who came by and hauled it away when Fran paid him $25. What if we had kept it all these years and had it reconditioned? It would be worth a lot more than $25. No, not really. More valuable is the sterling memory cherished these fifty-five years.

Tracking Seminole Patchwork in Florida

One muggy day in November, my daughter, Bel and I set out to find the skilled artisans of Seminole Patchwork. I had flown to Florida to spend Thanksgiving with Bel. Back home I was preparing to teach a Seminole Patchwork class after I returned and wanted an authentic look at the technique and the people. So here we were heading west, then south, and west again on the Tamiami Trail into flat, open grasslands and everglades. At last, we saw the sign for the Miccosukee Indian Village. The entrance was through a gift shop where we were told there were women sewing Seminole Patchwork strips.

Seminole Patchwork is created from long cloth strips (tabs) of different colors and widths. Different width tabs are sewn together forming a long strip. Then the long sewn together strip is cut a specific length and angle and rejoined in a certain order. The cut sections become small patches which are sewn together into a proscribed patterned strips that can be used to decorate garments, blankets and other items.

After entering the Village, we found ourselves on a pathway winding among thatch-roofed platforms called chickees which are traditional shelters used by the Seminoles in the Everglades. In one chickee, a woman sewed long tabs together on a portable electric sewing machine. She was wearing a skirt that hung down to her ankles. On her skirt, two horizontal bands of Seminole Patchwork were separated by bands of a darker solid color fabric and ornamented by many rows of rickrack. I watched her sew some long strips of small patches together to form the intricate bands like the ones that I saw on her skirt.

"How long does it take to make that?" I asked.

"About a week to do twenty yards," she replied, as she stitched on.

In the next chickee a young Seminole woman sat sewing while her five-month-old daughter slept perched in a cloth hammock above her head. The woman stitched solid color blue and gold tabs on her machine and intermittently rocked the baby by pulling a cloth tab attached to the hammock. She told me that she preferred cotton fabric and always tore it into tabs. She showed me some "old-fashioned" garments made by her mother, who taught her the technique. It was the ruffle on the bottom that made them old-fashioned she told me. She stood up to show me her waist-length cape, a gauze-like fabric with fullness gathered around the neck. There was no patchwork, but lace around the bottom, and many rows of rick rack above the lace. The young mother woke the baby to show off its dress. The dress was made in a mellow shade of indigo with an immense floral pattern and ruffles of blue and white print on the sleeves. Around the bodice, and midway down the skirt there was a band of red ribbon and a second band of white ribbon below the ruffle. What pride she showed in her heritage and her work!

As shadows got longer, we had to leave. Our safari to find Seminole Patchwork was a success. It was inspiring to see how well these women produced their patchwork in their traditional manner. Observing the authentic technique helped me to bring meaning to my Seminole Patchwork class.

Published in the Patchwork Patter, August 1989

Say No to Pollution

A murky atmosphere was my constant companion during a recent visit to Prague, Czechoslovakia. I saw sunlight just once and never enjoyed a star-studded sky at night. According to the January 2, 1992 McNeil-Lehrer News Hour, pollution in northern Czechoslovakia is the worst in Eastern Europe: things have become so bad that children are kept home from school and frequently do not go out to play. Abundant and conveniently available in the local mountains, brown coal is used for home heating, industry, and electrical power. The use of coal has become widespread since 1965, and it creates fumes that can be smelled and seen. The detrimental effects of the more than 25 years of air pollution are now becoming visibly evident. Forests of dead trees are visible on mountaintops. High rates of birth defects are being reported, and respiratory ailments are twelve times greater in Prague than for the rest of Czechoslovakia.

The few nuclear plants are obsolete and have, on several occasions, been on the verge of meltdown, so building more plants of the same design would not be practical. Curbing the environmental destruction and supplying the growing population with adequate energy is a monumental task facing a nation left a shadow of itself by the Russians, who, when they were departing left broken vehicles and spare parts resting in fields. They dumped oil, gas, and chemicals on the ground resulting in the contamination of groundwater. There seems to be no plan to clean up this mess. The growing of the Prague population, which has now reached 1.5 million, will make increasing demands on all resources.

The out-of-control pollution in Czechoslovakia is a belated legacy for future generations, a warning to the rest of the world, showing what happens when the environment is exploited. The quality of people's lives is diminished. There are dead trees on mountaintops. Offensive odors assail our nostrils. Over-fertilized golf courses push chemicals into groundwater where schools of dead fish have been found. Can we keep it from getting worse? Is this possible to clean up? Can Henderson County say no to pollution? Where in the world will we find the good Earth?

Canajoharie

During a recent trip to upstate New York, I had the opportunity to visit the Canajoharie Library and Art Gallery in Canajoharie, New York. Senator Arkel, who was the co-founder of a paper bag manufacturing company during the latter part of the nineteenth century, like other industrial tycoons of that time collected European art. He preferred paintings that reminded him of the scenic Mohawk Valley. His son Bartlett who became the first president of the Beech-Nut Packing Company inherited his father's art collection and was making his own collection of American Art.

In 1925, Arkell Bartlett presented the library and his father's art collection to the village of Canojoharie. By 1927, he added a gallery to the library in order to included his art collection. The fact that a gallery possessing a permanent collection of over 350 American paintings and sculptures exists in this rural setting is amazing, to say the least. An enlarged gallery was opened this year with state-of-the-art viewing access. Visitors now enter the gallery via a ramp from the library. Remote cameras monitored by the librarians provide surveillance. The gallery is lighted automatically as one enters the space and shuts off when there are no visitors. Changing exhibits feature works from the permanent collection year round, during library hours. An exhibition schedule is published annually. The collection includes the European art and American paintings. Works by Remington, Cassatt, Pendergast, Homer, Hassan and Whistler were on exhibit when I was there. There is enough artwork available from the storage area to make return visits worthwhile. Admission is free, but donations are accepted. Tours are available with a minimum of two-week advance notice; otherwise, the visit is self-guided.

This excursion was actually a return trip to a place I visited as a young child in the 1930's. My recollection has always been of the immense copy of the Night Watch by Rembrandt. It covered an entire wall and was overwhelming to one so young. More to my liking was the visit to the Beech-Nut factory across the street. I saw the molten mixture for Life Savers poured onto marble slabs and formed into that succulent sweetness. Best of all was the gift of a miniature cardboard suitcase filled with what appeared to be a lifetime supply of Life Savers.

The village of Canajoharie is located north of Cooperstown, which is well known for the Baseball Hall of Fame, the James Fennimore Cooper home, and the Farmer's Museum. It is only a mile from Exit 29 off the New York State Thruway. The unusual name stems from the early Indian dwellers' word for the many potholes formed in the Mohawk River by receding glaciers at the end of the ice age. If you time your visit right, Beech-Nut still offers tours to their plant. We were too late for a tour this time, so I wasn't able to find out if they still give out those miniature cardboard suitcases.

December 1995 Letter

To think that only 1% of US telephone owners have rotary phones – and I am one of them! Oh well, I did spend this past year trying out the information highway by taking computer classes at Blue Ridge Community College (BRCC). Fascinating, but I'm not ready to invest yet. I'll stick to my rotary phone and United States Postal Service for now. Do keep in touch.

This year was a big travel year for me. In February, we visited Dan and Edna in Florida and took a look at the Florida Panhandle. In July, I made a 2000-mile solo round-trip from Hendersonville to upstate New York. During this trip, I drove across the Chesapeake Bay Bridge and took a look at Falling Water in Pennsylvania on the way back. In late November, Fran and I drove the Natchez Trace, a lovely parkway, and, in December, we drove through the Alleghany Mountains of West Virginia and Pennsylvania. I returned south on Amtrak with a stop off in New York City, where I saw two shows and visited three museums in three days. Lots of good things to remember.

Now that I'm safely home, I'll be satisfied to pedal my bike around here for a while. I really enjoy biking, and in May, I rode my bike 45 miles for Diabetes over on Hatteras Island. I also rode 35 miles Labor Day weekend in the Apple Festival bike tour in the mountains. Don't be flabbergasted. It took me all day on the first and the better part of the second day to do it. Just one silly millimeter at a time.

My patchwork has been focused on "recaps" (caps made from neckties), and I started a drawing class at Blue Ridge Community College, in hopes that it will get me ready for wall hangings again. Let's see what '96 brings all of us. Perhaps heaps of PEACE for all humankind. Best for your health, hearth, and happiness in the New Year.

Cheers, Carla

Touring New York State Canals

"Don't you people know it's raining!" exclaims a sprightly woman from under her umbrella. We are huddled with our bikes under a maple tree in front of the Lockport, NY City Hall. This is the start of our New York State Canal bike trip. Not only is it raining, it's Friday the 13th. Fran and I have long planned this trip. We are committed to riding the canal bikeway whatever the weather. The previous afternoon while we feasted on delightful delicacies and cappuccino at the Holy Canoli bakery, we saw a plaster frieze hung high on the wall. It read Fede, Speranza, Amore, which translates to Faith, Hope, and Love. Perhaps, we thought, it is an omen that will successfully guide us on our journey.

Our moist beginning is with Speranza, Hope, as we wheel our bikes down the wet slope past the five locks of The Old Erie Canal. They look like giant water steps carved from the limestone rock of the Niagara Escarpment. Parallel to them are two larger locks built in 1918 when the canal was improved to carry 30,000 ton motorized barges that replaced the 3,000 ton mule drawn packet boats.

The bikeway we ride is on top of the berm, a dirt embankment helping to hold back the canal waters. It is above the level of the land and covered with fine crushed stone. We pass from town to countryside and see wet, level fields of young crops and peach orchards. Lake Erie to the West and Lake Ontario to the north moderate the climate and allow for a good growing season. Straight ahead, tall trees arch their branches over the trail. At intervals there are bridges spanning the canal. They are for intersecting roads that provide a crossing for vehicles, pedestrians, and bikers. Most boats are too tall to go under the bridges and boats have the right of way. When a boat approaches, the bridge is elevated and a barrier automatically blocks road traffic and pedestrians from entering the bridge at either end. Traffic waits when the Lift Bridge goes up and the boat passes.

There are signs and maps informing us about local history and geography as we near small towns along the bikeway. It is a land filled with natural resources from prehistoric times. Times when there were ancient seas that left limestone and red sandstone when they receded. When the Erie Canal was built limestone was quarried along Lake Ontario to build walls, aqueducts and locks for the canal. Fragments of that first canal can be seen today in pastures, wetlands and along the Thruway. We see large sandstone and limestone buildings standing in many of the towns and villages we pass. They are reminders of a-once-thriving canal commerce. Today, the canal carries pleasure boats between Albany on the Hudson and Buffalo on Lake Erie.

The rain ends by the time we reach the town of Medina. There are clusters of bright yellow iris at the water's edge and darting dragonflies skimming around puddles. Bird songs are in the air. We have a comforting hot lunch at a canal side restaurant. Then continue pedaling towards Albion where we will stay overnight. Not far from Medina is one of the wonders of the canal. For a short span, the canal becomes an aqueduct and allows a road to pass beneath it. We watch an approaching car on the far side disappear under the canal and then emerge below us on our side. Fishermen are out patiently trying their luck and savoring the afternoon tranquility.

After our B&B overnight, we bike to Rochester for the weekend with children and grandchildren. Sunday is sunny and the whole family rides the canal trail from Rochester to Palmyra. We stop off in Fairport at the Lift Bridge Restaurant for a buffet brunch. We eat outside overlooking the canal and watch the lift bridge being hoisted for some pleasure crafts. Swarms of people are out enjoying a stroll along the path, meeting friends, and sitting on benches licking dripping ice cream cones. It is a time filled with family, friends and Amore, Love.

After Palmyra the bikeway turns to the highway and traffic increases around Syracuse. So we choose to carry our bikes on the car as we continue east on the Thruway and head to Syracuse and a visit to the Erie Canal Museum. The Museum is in the Old Weigh Lock building on a very dry Erie Boulevard. At one time Erie Blvd. was the Erie Canal and went straight through the city center. The Weigh Lock was a device that allowed boats to be weighed. A toll was charged according to the tonnage on board. The museum contains many artifacts and historical data about the Old Erie Canal. We board and inspect a nineteenth century canal boat and get a sense of earlier canal travel.

Money for building the canal was first appropriated when Gov. Dewitt Clinton convinced a skeptical state legislature that a canal would benefit the state economically. Digging the canal, by hand, started on July 4,1817 at Rome, NY. It was named the Erie Canal, and was scornfully called 'Clinton's Ditch' until it was finished in 1825. The canal route followed the settlers' wagon path that traced the old Indian trail going west. If the canal crossed their land, farmers were responsible for digging that section of the canal. The 'ditch' was 40 feet wide at the top, 4 feet deep, and 28 feet wide at the bottom. On one side was a 5-foot wide berm and on the other side was a 12-foot wide towpath for mules that pulled the canal boats. It was an engineering marvel that crossed the center of the state for 363 miles from Albany on the Hudson River to Buffalo on Lake Erie.

Next we head for the Greenway along the Old Erie Canal between Dewitt and Rome. The bikeway leads us through a dark, swampy land populated by a multitude of croaking frogs. There are low-lying places filled with large ferns and hanging vines. This part of the bikeway is completely out of sight of any civilization. It winds through a foliage dense wetland scattered with remnants of the old canal filled with stagnant water and covered with mossy green algae. Remnants of limestone walls show where there were locks and aqueducts. The lock gates are gone and no boats navigate here. Flocks of Canada Geese hunker down on the path. They hiss and reluctantly make way for us.

About five miles before Rome, our path brings us to Lock #21 of the NY State Canal. Three small pleasure crafts are locking through on their way to Oneida Lake. They are deep in the trough of the lock when the gates are swung open and they go on their way. Water is either pumped in or out of a lock to enable boats to descend or ascend changes in elevation. The level of the canal in Buffalo where it enters lake Erie is 500 feet greater than at Albany where it meets the Hudson River. The canal has 35 locks along the way, with the highest lock at Little Falls. We ask the Lock Tender where we go to continue on the trail. He tells us the other side of the canal. We must cross the catwalk on top of the 15' high lock gate. My heart sinks. I'm dizzy and frightened. "Isn't there another way?" I plead. He says that it is the only way to continue. He offers to refill the lock so the surface of the water will be closer. He pushes a button on the control device in his hand; the huge doors clang shut, and water bubbles up inside the lock. I take a deep breath and summon up 'Fede,' Faith in myself to inch across looking only at the water in the canal. My bike and I reach the other side. I feel good about my accomplishment and better to be back on Terra Firma.

We end the first part of our trip in Rome, NY where the first spade full of dirt for the Erie Canal was dug 186 years ago. It was the willing spirit of the colonial settlers of varied cultures and religions who labored to dig the Erie Canal. It not only benefited the people of those times, it left a legacy of cooperation, neighborliness and a free accessible thoroughfare. Today the New York State Canalway Trail offers biking and walking along the canal for all people to enjoy. It is place to see engineering marvels, historic places, the countryside, neighbors and friends and maybe have a refreshing ice cream. For us it has been a trip filled with Speranza, Feda and Amore.

The Promised Land

It would be a lie to say the transition for the Rodios from South to North was a smooth flowing event. However, our passage from North Carolina through Tennessee on into Virginia, West Virginia, Maryland, Pennsylvania and finally New York was a feast for our eyes. Every turn in the road revealed muted colors of the fall trees on the mountainsides. The lack of rain created this effect. We went to Utica so we could go to Cooperstown for Fran's medical procedure on 10/28. On 10/29, Fran had a setback, but by 10/31, Fran was well enough for me to leave him in the care of friends and head for Rochester.

Our furniture and over fifty boxes we had packed were due there on November 2nd, and I needed to see the apartment we had rented. The weather had turned cold and it was Halloween. I found the apartment complex in Pittsford most appealing. The place was set back away from the major roads. I could see the pathway to the Canal trail, too. The manager welcomed me and took me to see the apartment. Now this is the spooky part on this Halloween day. I had been told that the apartment had been newly painted and new carpeting installed. When the landlord unlocked the door, a certain odor came to my nostrils and choked in my throat. As I was being walked through the place tears gushed from my eyes. What was this awful smell? I suspected it might be formaldehyde which had at one time been used to make cloth wash and wear and other fibers stain resistant and of course to embalm the deceased. Even though its use has been outlawed in fibers, it can be used in the glue to install carpeting. I knew if we stayed more than ten minutes in that place the undertaker would have his work done for him. But what to do?

Sue got in touch with another place she and Rob really liked better. It was still available. We were able to see it even though it was Sunday. Monday morning I signed the lease. Our mover arrived on Tuesday. Whew! Here we are on the 11th floor of a high rise overlooking rooftops, treetops, and Amtrack's main line, through large picture windows. The windows make the place light and bright. In the basement there is an exercise room, coffee and bagels in large dining area every Mon morning, a library room with books and gas logs, screening room where films are shown every Wed. and Sat., a green house, raised beds outside to plant summer vegetables and laundry room with Maytag washers. Outside sidewalks are everywhere. A block and a half away is a Wegmans grocery and in the other direction is a discount grocery twice the size of GO. Everyday there are new discoveries. Leaves are still on the trees here. In fact, there has not been a hard frost, but I'm sure winter is not far off.

I can't help missing the mountains, riding my bike on country roads, and friends who were like family. Good memories stored. Time to take out the poems and essays, sort them and try putting them together. I must consider contrasts, textures, direction and meaning in putting words and thoughts together. Like making a wall hanging. It will be a new way to use what I have learned in creating my newest piece of work.

Recap

wearable art

IX

End Notes

City Scape

wall hanging

The Highway of Life

For all the highway of life is not always smooth.
More bumpy for some than others.
There are detours and potholes for all travelers.
The road never runs straight and smooth.
Finding your way is all part of the journey.

The Last Words

The purpose for this book was to create a legacy for family, friends and interested spectators. It is comprised of wall hangings, poems and essays created during my mid-life, a time of self-discovery and learning for me. I wanted to make a diverse collection of writings and patchwork into a meaningful tapestry of thoughts, experiences and creations. It was May Kedney's words, "to keep the faculty of effort trained", that helped me to make sense out of what seemed much of the time like an impossible task.

As a quilter, I joined together a variety of cloth scraps in a significant way. I worked on a flannel-covered wall. The scraps of fabric would cling to the flannel so I could step back and look at the composition. I began to wonder if odd pieces of writing could be made to look as harmonious as a quilt top. Instead of using the color or shape of fabric pieces, I grouped the document into what seemed like a shared meaning or theme. My hope is to have each poem and story relate to its section of the book as closely as possible. Each book section is like a quilt block. The computer screen became my canvas where I could look at each document and see how it related to others. Together, all the sections make the book. Now, when I step back, I see a colorful blanket of words woven together with expression, direction and harmony. This is my mid-life story of finding myself. It is my satisfaction to share it with you.

Preparing this book could not have been managed without the help of some very special people. Quilt design classes with Michael James and Nancy Crow taught me to push beyond tradition in making patchwork wall hangings. I couldn't have finished some of my wall hangings without Carol Sambora's skill with the quilting needle. It was Susan Snowden's writing classes and her encouragement that started me to take my writing seriously. My longtime friend and computer guru, Sue Mahnken, kept my computer and I compatible through crashes and mysterious deletions and losses. Renée Schuls-Jacobson, guided me through the difficult, complicated steps needed to prepare this book for publication. Katie Wright at Scott's Photo helped me select slides of my quilts for the book's publications. Howard Levant lent his professional skills to format the book cover and photos. I was fortunate to have long-term friends like Katie and Steve Breckheimer. The Senior Writers group meetings at Writers and Books kept me focused and supported. Fran Rodio read every page for grammar and spelling mistakes.

It has been a wonderful journey working with so much encouragement. I couldn't have done it alone. Cheers to all and those who patiently waited for me to reconnect.

There are no failures.
Insights come through experiences.

Patchwork Index

0. *Las Montanas* ©1997, book cover, silk necktie scraps

1. *Along the Mohawk* ©1986, part of Sea to Shining Sea Banner for Great American Quilt Festival, published in Quilts Across America, exhibited across America

2. *Nebula* ©1985, kite crafted and hand painted

3. *Splendor* ©1983, cotton broadcloth, published in *Half Square Triangles* ©1987, Barbara Johanna

4. *A Quilt for All Ages* ©1987, cotton print scraps

5. *Six Million Stars* ©1993, scrap wool fabric tied with buttons

6. *Henderson County Earth Day Quilt* ©1991, Author with Carol Sambora

7. *New Horizon* ©1988, pile fabric wall hanging

8. *New Horizons 3* ©1989, pile fabrics, wall hanging

9. *Four Seasons* ©1991, cotton and cotton blends,

10. *Sparklers* ©1983, cotton fabric and batting, hand quilting by Carol Sambora, Published in Contemporary Quilts p.53

11. *Log Cabin/House Variation* ©1987, cotton broadcloth, tied

12. *Appalachian Trails #2 ½* ©1985, cotton cloth and batting, wall hanging

13. *Triptych* ©1984, fabric stained glass technique

14. *Appalachian Trails #2* ©1985, hand quilting by Carol Sambora, Cooperstown Art Association Annual 1986 (Second Prize),WNCQG Harvest of Quilts 1987 (first prize), Sixth Annual Smokey Mountain Quilt Show (Honorable Mention), published in Half Square Triangles

15. *Recap* ©1992, fashioned from men's neckties for wearable art

16. *City Scape-Empire State Series* ©1998, velvet and corduroy, wall hanging

17. Author portrait

About the Author

Carla Rodio lives in Upstate New York where she has been working on preparing many of her poems, essays and quilts for publication in her book, Patchwork Scrapbook. Some of her poems and stories as well as pictures of her quilts have been published in periodicals and books. Many of her quilts have been exhibited in Juried and Invitational shows nationally and locally. She has taught in The Mountain Arts Program in Western North Carolina; at the John C. Campbell Folk Art School; Appalachian Center for Crafts; Munson Williams Proctor Institute; Owned and Managed Quilters Comfort quilt shop; Taught Adult Literacy and Elementary School. In 1988, the Henderson County Arts Council awarded her an Emerging Artist grant. In 1990, she received a Grass Roots Grant to prepare The Earth Day Quilt for permanent exhibition.

70839822R00061

Made in the USA
Columbia, SC
15 May 2017